THE BOUNDLESS GOD

ADRIENNE VON SPEYR

THE
BOUNDLESS
GOD

Translated by Helena M. Tomko

IGNATIUS PRESS   SAN FRANCISCO

Original German edition:
Der Grenzenlose Gott
© 1955, Johannes Verlag, Einsiedeln

Cover design by Roxanne Mei Lum

© 2004 Ignatius Press, San Francisco
All rights reserved
ISBN 978-0-89870-996-4
Library of Congress control number 2003115826
Printed in the United States of America ∞

For Werner

CONTENTS

I

CREATION

From all eternity, the Father is together with the Son and with the Holy Spirit. He reveals himself to them in a way that is completely divine and receives from them a divine answer. Nonetheless, when the Father created the world, he opened wide the sphere of the eternal in order to include within existence the sphere of the transient as well. He set forth something from his eternity, though not in order to leave what he had created without a connection to eternity, as a unity left to its own devices. God also received what he had created and, therefore, preserved a permanent relationship with his work. His will as Creator remained unchanged with respect to the world, and, in the act of creation, the Creator's being was disclosed to the world. He neither withdrew nor became indifferent, but rather he waited for an answer from the created.

His creation's first answer was to let itself be created, to let itself become a reality, one whose ultimate meaning was meant to rest in God but that also possessed meaning in its creaturely essence. God separated the water from the dry land, and, in this separation, the earth became an important symbol. The earth is the sure ground on which men can stand. For everything was planned for man, whom God created last of all. He handed over everything to him so that it would belong to him. This handing over was meant with the utmost sincerity and was never revoked. It placed man in a permanent relationship with the surrounding world, which was God's gift to him. In God's eyes, occupying man in this way was meant already to be like a prayer, for man was meant to see in created things what God had given him. He was to be able to do this by virtue of his senses and reason, in what he saw, heard, felt, and experienced. He was furnished with a sensory nature and with knowledge, and, through these, he can echo and adjust to the things over which he has dominion. However, God stands behind each and every perception and adjustment. This means, not that God allows himself to be restricted or tied down to the measure of things and experiences, but rather that his voice remains always audible. The more simple things are, the more conceivable God appears. It is not that he allows things to contain him; rather, they are signs of his presence, which can be neither diminished by the finitude of the world nor consigned to a particular space; it nonetheless remains true presence. This presence is something neither vague nor questionable: it is the presence of the Creator toward whom points the meaning that resides in created things. It is not that God's meaning is made finite in elements, in plants, and in animals, like something exhaustible; but things can be either quiet or loud reminders that the invisible Creator lives, has created them, and, far from abandoning them, has them permanently in his care. The human spirit, which experiences and contemplates these things, is reminded by their presence of God's existence.

The first beginnings of man's relationship with God lie in his relationship to things and to the hidden powers and secrets with which God has invested them for man's sake. Man is appointed as the lord of creation. He is to be permanently concerned with the things of this world in order to make them bend to his will and so to remain faithful to God's command and adjust to what God expects of him. But, through his growing knowledge of, and dominion over, things, he experiences that an infinite divine knowledge must stand hidden behind them; for the things themselves neither contain God nor betray his ultimate mysteries. They are scattered testimonies and hints that function as such because they are ordered to the searching and questioning of the human spirit. They are created for man to such an extent that they need him in order for their meaning to be revealed. It is therefore understandable that, throughout the millennia, man has never reached the point of being done with the earth and is shown, in ever new forms of work, things and laws that were always in existence in the world but that, having been revealed, lent a related historical meaning to subsequent generations of men. Man, who is created for the honor of God, also honors the Creator through his growing insight into the meaning that God has placed in things, a meaning that is unveiled slowly through the ages. This is the process that one tends to call progress, providing it is not divorced from the intentions of the Creator. Man should work and explore, not for the sake of mere domination and the power that comes with it, but rather in order to remain within the sphere of tasks assigned to him by God.

In addition to creating the earth, God created the sea, which he separated from the dry land and which remains a particularly eloquent symbol for the strength, mystery, and perpetual unfathomableness of God. Man will want to understand more and more about the sea as well and will probably be able to do so. And yet, the sea remains a special object of contemplation: its relative boundlessness and sameness in all its waves and change provides an allegory for God. When a human being surveys the sea, he looks into something unpredictable, something no longer finite; he experiences that behind everything he sees and intuits there is something "ever farther"; and when he alters his vantage point, this "farther" proves to be essentially the "same" as what he already knows. Whereas God created the earth to be hard and sandy, rocky and lush, fertile and covered in age-old ice, he gave to the sea, in all its raging depths, a quality of uniformity: sea water is the same everywhere, and though no wave is ever identical to another, all waves are nonetheless similar and emerge from and into one another. But it is not just in contemplation of, but also in the struggle against, the sea that human beings are reminded urgently of God. Even if man manages to overcome the sea, he never feels he has mastered the element. Man is conscious of his mastery of terrestrial things: he can plough his fields as he sees best, just as his predecessors did; he can increase or impede the fertility of the land. Of course, man remains a mere servant of God even in this, since God either sends or denies the harvest. But God's predominance emerges more clearly in the image of the sea. Man can navigate it and catch its fish but cannot direct or cultivate it. Each wave tells him this; storm and stillness proclaim it to him, and both are allegories and reminders that provoke more profound reflection and enable him to be detached from himself, his own might, and his boundaries. In surveying the sea, a person who is accustomed to praying can recognize how much of himself God betrays through the sensory world, how loudly he calls and exhorts men, and how clearly he reveals his love of creation, which is as alive today as it was on the first day.

All that has been created should be experienced as a communication from God, above all of his greatness and his infinity. The one who creates is greater than his work. Should we try, in faith, to consider this work as the Father does but not get very far with the help of reason, we can try to do so with the help of love. Our own love, however, is not sufficient: what we, as believers, call love is at the most a poor likeness of that which God calls love. For this reason, God has disclosed to us his own love, and faith teaches us, not just to see this love, but to live in it. The more firmly we believe, the more profoundly we learn how to live out of love, not out of our love, but out of God's love, which can overwhelm us again and again because it is his. Even faith itself, through which we gain access to this love, is a gift of the triune God for us; and through faith we acquire a meaning for the Father's love hidden in things. In order to encounter this love, we must not limit our reflections to the divine proofs of love that we find in the Old and New Testaments; rather, we may dare to wonder at God's love in the creation that lies spread out before us.

The Father's action—which creation obviously seems to be—can be understood as the fruit of his eternal contemplation. He has divided his work into "days", thereby conforming himself to transient time, which he will give to us as our habitat, in order therein to separate and bring forth. This is already a sign of his love. He takes what he creates as his very own and fills it with what is his; his love moved him to make days that could be counted, and he places an infinite hope in them, for he does not find them good in some remote way; rather, he fills them with his own goods. If today we have doubts about the worth of our temporal, fleeting lives, we should look back to the magnificence of the first days, to each of which God gave its own mark, a unique content, up to and including the Sabbath, the day of the great contemplation of everything that had been done, a contemplation that God wanted to give to us as well. When Christ says, "You, therefore, must be perfect, as your heavenly Father is perfect", the possibility of this imitation rests on the perfection of the days of the world that God has created, days so good that they can become days divinely fulfilled through his love.

Not only the perfection of the created days but also the readiness of eternal life to support creaturely life in love are shown in the fact that God can make immediate use of those days. There is already a prelude in the first phase of the plan to what the Son of God will do for men when he, having become man, makes our days his own. The outline is already visible of the bridge that the Son will build from eternal life into transient time.

God uses the "days" in order further to create: he brings forth plants, animals, and, finally, man. These all proceed from his creating hand in a completeness that he himself begets by acknowledging everything to be very good. His contemplation now appears twofold: it is a reflection and judgment of creation; and he gives both forms of contemplation to us because they both convey something of God's essence. As Creator, he can only create good and does not let it run away from him; rather, he keeps it within his sight and judgment—that is, in a loving relationship to him.

Although these things are so very good, God gives them to man. He does not, however, talk to things: his first word is intended for man. Since we know that the Son is the Word who dwells with the Father, we also understand that, in addressing man, the Father establishes an initial relationship between the Son and man. Christians will experience through John that the word in Genesis was already a gift to them from the Father: a promise of the Son, who will some day become one among us, to the world. We can therefore understand ourselves as having come into being from the hand of the Father and into the Son's Spirit. Our sinful life, however, seems like a sad interlude belonging to us alone, an interlude the Father did not want and for which the Son makes amends. Anything that we do not live in faith and obedience to the Father, Son, and Spirit shrivels into an episode that is bracketed between the love of the Creator and that of the Redeemer. From the outset, therefore, we can say that God's mercy towers above our existence—above everything to which we can imagine this existence amounts—and that this mercy is given to the created world as its own.

The rest for contemplation on the seventh day is the Father's rest in the Son and in the Holy Spirit. Just as the Son possesses the vision of the Father during his life on earth, so too does the Father possess the presence of the Son and Spirit during his creation and his rest. His triune life is neither altered nor interrupted by the creation. The Father shows, through the words he directs at men and through his confirmatory judgment, just how close the Son and Spirit already are to man and how greatly they share in the Father's work; so much so that the Incarnation of the Son and the sending forth of the Spirit are already contained and decreed invisibly in the visible work of creation. This is, therefore, the work of the one triune God, begun by the Father, who marks out, so to speak, the tasks whose execution will meantime not be fully transparent to us. The Son will use this divine communion as a model when he establishes the communion of saints. He will make of the Church a house into which he will invite the Father and the Spirit and into which he will send the Spirit, who lives in eternity with him and with the Father.

God stands in a threefold relationship with the first man: he is his Creator; he is his Father; he has made him into his image and likeness. As Creator, he has erected a great work, which in no way exhausts his power but rather leaves him free to take further measures as he sees best. But even his first work of creation imparts some idea of his superior grandeur, and thus the first time that man has someone whom he can address as "you", it is the Creator, a God who cares for him and who emerges as his Father by establishing this first primordial relationship. This is a relationship between the sublime and the negligible, between the mighty and the lowly. The relationship contains man's likeness to God, and man knows this. He is aware of embodying things that are the Creator's and the Father's. Man embodies an idea of the Father, and, when God appoints him to be lord over all created things, he initiates man into the mysteries of his fatherhood, sharing a power with him that originates from his own and furnishing him with these created things just as the Father has furnished himself with man. He has created things for men just as he created man for himself.

But it is not as something hopelessly finite that man, the image and likeness of God, confronts the infinite archetype, almost as if he were the last finite being at the end of a chain of finite beings. And even though man renounces the heavenly archetype when he sins, the Son of God will raise the end of the chain to heaven, for he will be both God and man and, on earth, will show to us a no less perfect image and likeness of the Father than he was in heaven from eternity. Though man will cloud his own image and likeness through sin and will distance himself increasingly from God, the Son will restore the image to its proper place—the place originally indicated to him by the Father—through his perfect accord and consubstantiality with the Father. Through his Incarnation, he will point to the Father and to his own divine being, not from a sublime height far above us, but in his life among us and in his staying with us permanently in the Eucharist, just as he stays and abides with the Father in heaven. He does not merely once and for all put the image back into its correct place in relation to its archetype, the Father; rather, he remains permanently efficacious among us even after his return to the Father: he is the living leaven who makes us rise up to the archetype. He may well bring creation more or less to a close upon his return to heaven, for on earth he has shown the Father the perfect human being. But, at the same time, he remains in his brothers, the children of the Father, in order to care for them and, in them, to show to the Father what he himself is. Though man may still feel greatly overwhelmed by the distance of guilt separating him from God, he now knows— almost against his will and ability—that he has to be the image of God, at least in his gift of self to the Son and lack of resistance to him who can recreate the image within him. However, when the Son proves himself capable of this, he makes it clear that he has also created together with the Father, that the character of creation is equally and originally his, and that, in assuming fallen man unto himself, he enters into a territory he has forever known and ruled. For the first Adam, the Son remained hidden in the Father, yet the Son knew that he was meant to become the second Adam. Therefore, the fact that he hid himself in the Father was already proper to the mystery of his Incarnation. Since the Father can only be seen in heaven, and no one has seen the Father except the Son, the Son revealed and showed himself so that man might become newly attentive to the Father's divinity through what was divine in him—though without attempting to separate Father and Son along this path of mediation: the Son wants to be the door and the entrance through whom the open vision of the Father is unveiled.

II

OVERCOMING HUMAN FINITUDE

When God creates the world he makes a beginning right in the middle of his eternity, a beginning that inaugurates the realm of number and numeration; day and night are already separated, and so times are placed in rhythmic succession. The work is complete on the sixth day; but by spending the seventh day at rest, God shows that the cessation of his work does not mean that he is terminating the relationship he has begun or withdrawing into heaven, and most certainly not that he is turning away from created man. The realm of number and of finitude does not close in on itself; it remains the arena of infinite, that is, eternal life. And when we are told that the Father is in communion with the Son and with the Spirit from eternity, we also experience that he is a God of love who begets the Son as his image and likeness, who pours out the Spirit, and who lets them both participate in the same eternity and infinity while receiving from them this very same eternity and infinity. Love thus knows no bounds; it proceeds from and to the eternal God. When God directs his love toward men, however, he does not invent a new quality of love. The final judgment of "very good" contains the fact that the creature exists within sight of God's eternal love—this is creature as the work of God and untouched, as yet, by sin.

Because man sins and becomes unworthy of God's love, God creates a punishment while at the same time also creating—as a new testimony of love—that which alone can be identified as the experience of finitude in the actual sense: he creates death. Through death, God puts an end to the creature who has chosen sin so that the condition of being in sin does not continue without bounds. This imposed end is both punishment and mercy and bears the insoluble stamp of a divinely imposed measure that from the outset looks forward to the coming redemptive death of the Son. Were man, as he has become, to continue his life on earth without end, his would be a completely ineluctable situation. He would have become a sinner once and for all, a sinner unable to find a way back to God. However, a way back does present itself in two interconnected ways: through grace in mortal life and through grace in death. God's grace can touch a living sinner: he converts, puts an end to sin through God's grace, and lives the remainder of his life in grace, though in the knowledge that God has marked an end for all human beings in death. The convert will stride through death as one who was already been touched by grace in life and who will find in death the God of love. But this is only true because the Son has taken upon himself the end that is death and has died for all men, including this particular convert. Because the Son dies for and with him, he will be entrusted in death completely to the grace of God. Therefore, he already knows in life that the finitude of his existence corresponds to a grace from God that has been granted to all men and not just to him. The experience of his finitude, however, affords him knowledge of God's infinity: his knowledge of the end of earthly life is a recognition of eternal life. He can thus regard death, not only as punishment, but equally as the Father's grace. The Son has taken death's purely punitive character upon himself and thereby released the character of grace for his brothers, whereby he unveils and fulfills the purpose of finitude. He also does this for those who did not experience the grace of conversion in life, who die in ignorance, and who would be delivered in complete helplessness to the end imposed by God had the Son, by dying, not drawn heaven closer to them. On earth they do not yet know of this realm; they only discover its existence having passed through death. In a way, they are the saints of the very last hour who are given insight only after it is already too late from an earthly perspective. For the Son's gift of self has broken the bounds of finitude for all, and the sign of this is his Resurrection from the dead. His descent into the underworld is part of this sign: he does not just pass fleetingly through these areas

unknown to us; he stays there for three days. He therefore takes the entire accumulation of his strength
into the sacrifice that led to his death, beyond death
and into the underworld. He lets himself take effect
there so as to crown the act of redemption and open
to sinners a previously unsuspected form of being
struck by his presence. Since the Son became man
and kept company with us in our form, we claim
to know what this form was. Nonetheless, for each
word he spoke, for each miracle he performed, and
most properly at his death and Resurrection, we have
to allow for dimensions that we cannot master intel-
lectually; the world that he brought with him is his
heavenly world, the world of the Father and of the
Spirit, a world that infinitely surpasses our own. As
humans, we are inclined to regard each act that the
Son performs as finite, yet with each act he opens
up infinity. Each time he does something as man,
he does something divine. In everything he is and
does, he grants us glimpses into the boundlessness
of heaven. These strengthen our faith and, what is
more, are capable of increasing our hope and love.
For these are acts from the center of God's infinite
love, which are not only surrounded by the Father's
love and not only point to it but also have the characteristic of including us and almost throwing us into
his love.

Confession grants us just such a view of infinity.
When we go to confession, we pass through a kind

of death and, by acknowledging our sin, reach the end of it—the end that God has instituted through death. We repentantly confess and reach a boundary, an endpoint given us by the Son. The absolution we receive comes from beyond the here and now and is comparable to going to heaven. Sin is shown its end in accordance with God's punitive judgment, but a new life is also shown its beginning. Man experiences through this that God is exercising his love anew. He has been granted death and confession so that he can grant new space to the infinite love of the triune God.

~

After the first fall from grace, God called the guilty man and spoke with him. The improbable occurs as the eternal instigates a dialogue with the transient in spite of man's turning away from God. This dialogue is the origin of *prayer*. People who pray have the constant opportunity to address God in such a way that their human finitude gains a share in God's infinity and experiences a response from eternity. God has gone yet farther. Through his Incarnation, the Son has invited believers to follow him and to live a life of intimacy with him. For as long as the Son dwells on earth, the apostles share his life, while the Son abides in the life of the Father as he communicates his life to the apostles. The Son is thus the mediator.

For his followers, discipleship means a life, not only alongside the Son, but at the heart of his life. It is thus no longer—as in the Old Testament—the life of the just and the prophets who were faced with an ever-hidden, invisible God at some unbridgeable remove. It is now coexistence with the Son in the Father's realm of life. In his earthly life, the Son embodies the meeting point between finitude and infinity. He, who has a perfect share in the life of the Father, allows man to share in it in the form of discipleship. The disciples live this through the word of the Son: they experience immediately that which he wants to say to them—which is also the mystery of the triune God. This is more than what prayer meant in the pre-Christian world—an act raised up from quotidian earthly life through which the believer seeks to reach the world of the heavenly God. Discipleship means living and staying without interruption in companionship and dialogue with God. Words formed in prayer receive new significance, as does, above all, contemplation and—perhaps still more so—the attitude of saying Yes in general. With his open Yes, a person invited to be a disciple receives a place within infinity already while on earth; his interests and everything that occupies him are intimately connected to God's plan; everything he does is directed toward this plan; he dedicates his entire life to the connections between these divine intentions; in return, he receives the assurance of carrying out the Father's will. Whenever he carries it out imperfectly, burdened and inhibited by his all too human nature, he also has the assurance that the Son will take on, and make up for, any shortcomings on his behalf until these do, in the end, correspond to the Father's will. The plan in which man now lives is a plan from eternity. This means that his spirit is caught up in the Spirit of God and, therefore, that the Holy Spirit lends support as mediator in order to unite man with the Son. For the duration of the Son's dwelling on earth, man saw what he did, experienced his miracles and his words. Had the Son not sent the Spirit, the believer might easily have been able to believe that the Son, endeavors of faith, indeed, all Christian existence were finite. But the Son sent the Spirit from eternal into human life laden, not only with the divine responsibility that characterizes the Spirit, but also with the gift of strengthening faith and all the other gifts of eternity. Because of this, believers henceforth truly live in the infinity of the Father. Each and every prayer lives from this; each and every human word of prayer is spoken out of finitude in order to be taken up into infinity. And it is not the number of prayers that determine the number of the soul's encounters with God. Rather, God affords to each prayer an expansive realm of effect and elevates the entire person at prayer into the atmosphere of eternity, even when this is far from imagined while the person is praying. The commandment of love that man has received from the Son will, above all, have the effect of drawing him into the atmosphere of prayer, because an act of mediation is required of the actual person praying, an act that is proper to the Son's act of mediation, because the person praying is a part of his love.

~

When God plans, he does so in his omniscience, which has always existed and surveys the whole of eternity. His plan takes eternity as the realm of permanence. Human beings plan wholly for the short term. It is to be expected of the nonbeliever that, in the best-case scenario, he will make plans that encompass the duration of his life. He thinks over what he has done and built hitherto, and he can conceive and build upon the plan in such a way as to develop it toward a particular goal that is well within the bounds of what is humanly possible. But man knows full well, if he is reasonable, that he is not protected against the accidents of what he calls fate. He can at least construct a "best-case scenario", and, if he lives long enough and his plans are sufficiently modest, he may experience its realization. In contrast, the believer only plans within a framework that signifies, "If it so pleases God." In the end, the believer who devotes his entire life to the service of God plans exclusively within God's plan. Were the framework to disappear, so too would the boundary of his own life; for this reason he allows God to put him where he will and then does what God demands of him, even if he has not the slightest guarantee of ever living to see the attainment of his personal plans. He understands very soon that what he does is not a beginning; the beginning lies in God. If he belongs to a religious community, he knows that he is continuing a tradition. He can solve a certain task, like writing a particular book or founding an establishment. But the plan of the actual thing lies so completely in God that any one of his confreres of the same intellectual and spiritual orientation might be able to continue the work. His life passes like a prayer whose formation has been entrusted to God: faith and love replace human plans. Of course, this does not mean that he ceases to think and look ahead. He knows, however, that God has received his life and assumed responsibility for the gift that he has given in entrusting his existence to God.

The prophets of the Old Testament are one of the best examples for how believers plan. God permanently leads their life in a visible way, but he also shakes it up in a visible way. Had Elijah or Elisha formed his own life plans, these would constantly have to have been destroyed by God himself. The believer in the New Testament, who devotes himself completely to God and chooses discipleship as his life's meaning, plans in direct dependence on the Son, who has said: "But of that day and hour no one knows." These words elucidate the inability of the devout Christian to plan. A connection between not planning and prayer now becomes visible; the one lives from the other. Not planning is related to the Church's treasury of prayer; it is the renunciation, in favor of God, of one's own guidance of daily events, just like a prayer that does not cling to a specific, confined form, a prayer that demands no specific fulfillment from God and can be accepted and fulfilled by him as it pleases him. Both participate respectively in the eternal life of God.

Whenever the current members of an existing religious order take over from a previous generation the furthering of a set goal, a continuity of the heritage results that is far stronger than it would be in a natural family. For a father may well direct his child during his lifetime, but the child will do his own will once he is grown. A good many people will build up a business and dream about how their grandchildren will continue it; but the family may die out before then or the son already have demands of his own. But when the demands are those of God, continuity is ensured; for the eternal God does not upset his own plans, and his connection to the world cannot be destroyed by human hands. What the nonbeliever regards as fate belongs to God's providence, and man can force no twist or break or any finitude upon it. In nature, continuity can be broken again and again; but this is not true of supernature. Reason may impose or presuppose continuity in nature, yet time and again continuities will be broken. In supernature, the plan always exists in its completeness and cannot be interrupted in any way.

III

ETERNAL AND TRANSIENT TIME

God has given his infinite measure to eternal time. There is not the slightest possibility of the believer taming God's measure in eternity by means of some human measure. The believer can, therefore, come at it only in a roundabout way, through God, that is, he reserves an as yet undefined space in his deepening image of God for that which is eternal time. Nonetheless, he must concern himself with eternal time; for eternal time is God's time, and all that is God's should never cease to preoccupy him as a believer. He must also attend to it because eternity is one form of the permanence in which he is to gain a share. He will attain to God's eternity out of his own transient time; that is a gift that originates from the Son's time of transience, from the time he borrowed from our time for his human existence. This establishes the relationship. Indeed, it was founded even earlier when the eternal God created transient time. It is just that we happen to have sinned in this time, though we know there is no room for sin in eternity. Through sin we have turned our transient time into a time that is bound for death. It is no

longer possible for us to imagine transience without death. If we wanted to try and think of a sinless
counterimage to our time we would have to look
immediately to eternity. Thus, we can only come
closer to grasping either time or eternity through
the relationship of the one to the other.

When within Christ's commandment of love we
single out a person with the intention of loving him
in a special way—and perhaps even of drawing closer
to God through this love—we try to see above all
else the good in this person. This would be easy if
the person were a saint, because the image he would
present would be one of such purity that we would
know, whenever we saw him, that what he reflected
was alien to our transient time and must therefore
come from another time that is not transient. When
we honor saints, look at their images, or endeavor to
catch something of their innermost thoughts, when
we pray with their words of prayer or seek to imitate their composure, we experience that what constitutes their mission, and what they have to give
to the world, does not belong to this time. They
represent something that they draw from eternity,
from proximity to the Father and from the eternal
dialogue of the Divine Persons, in order to mediate
it to the world. This image attains its fulfillment in
the Son, who, as God, has brought divine eternity
to earth and concludes his life by redeeming us from
transient time into eternal time through suffering as

he bears our sins, erasing our guilt and cleansing our souls before God. In doing so, he makes our souls fit for eternity, though he alone remains the permanent origin and place of this characteristic. If we were to consider ourselves, we would forever quickly be running into things that were irreconcilable with the Son's gift of eternity. Thus, amid our faults and sins we can never achieve a proper estimation of the relations of both transient and nontransient time. In relative terms, it is easiest to attain the correct image by considering the saints. A good many traits are common to them all: love of God, adoration of the Incarnate, invocation of the Spirit, a constant yearning for the next life, and a hunger that cannot be satiated by this or that piece of information but that rather demands the presence of God. And when God satiates this hunger by giving himself to them as bread and wine, the Holy Mass brings, not an earthly Christ to them, but rather the Body of *God*, a Body that comes from and lives in eternity. The Son has instituted the Eucharist in such a way that the priest's words of transubstantiation, in accordance with the complete intention of the Church, cause the bread and wine to become the Body and Blood of Christ. The Church is, therefore, in the position to form, at Christ's command, the transition between heaven and earth and to give our transient, bodily life something of the eternal God, whenever our body is inhabited by a believing, loving soul that wants to receive heaven on earth and lets the eternal live in the midst of our transience.

~

God has not just brought snippets of heavenly existence to earth in the sacraments, nor has he just given the faithful a hint of, or rather a sense of reality for, the existence of a heavenly world: he has actually elevated the faithful right into eternity. He gives a new dimension to their entire endeavor, to their way of judging things and to their hopes. This dimension is a fulfillment that resides in God himself from which they now nonetheless already win something of a foretaste of their nontransience in him. This is not a fitful shuttling to and fro between heaven and earth, but a quiet growth on earth into the world of heaven; heaven is not revealed in such a way as to divulge itself completely all at once. When Stephen saw heaven open, this did not mean that he was transported without a transition from the reality of earth into the reality of heaven; rather, he already had an essential share in heaven through his faith. On earth he lived as one entrusted with a heavenly task at the end of which was martyrdom, but he had himself already learned to distinguish between what is heavenly in essence and what is earthly in essence. His martyrdom did indeed mean for him the conclusion of his earthly witness of faith, but precisely this end opened up for others something of the heavenly world that has no end. The vision of heaven for which he was stoned was the high point of his witness; it was the world to which he had pointed becoming visible, God's kept promise of eternity.

The reality of the sacraments therefore has a two-fold effect for the faithful. It lets them grow deeper into eternal life; it makes the earthly foreign; and it makes the heavenly home. On the other hand, it affords a new meaning to earthly things for those who must still dwell on earth: they learn to separate the essential from the unimportant, to direct and transform earthly things into that which is essential, thus giving them their share in the eternal. In both regards, each Holy Communion mediates the believer's coming closer to the eternal Lord: it is in no sense a one-sided movement of the Lord toward man. Each time, man becomes more capable of understanding God and committing himself to him in obedience and love.

This can also be considered with respect to Christ. When he is living in obedience to the Father on earth, and the Father determines his path from heaven, the Son responds by accepting this path in love and doing in love what the Father desires. This something is eternal, in accordance with the Son's origin and his very substance. For the people who follow him, this means that they orient themselves in loving obedience toward the eternal and let themselves be raised from temporality into eternity. The result is the reevaluation of all earthly things. What man is and has, what he experiences in and around himself in the transient world, what he loses, his wealth and impoverishment: in the sight of heaven, all these things attain a completely different significance. Stephen does not complain about his death and does not once talk about it; dying is insignificant to him in the face of the opened heavens. Accordingly, all that is transient in man and in his environment becomes provisional and representative, and it must make room for the eternal at the hour appointed by God. The nonbeliever, for whom death signifies a radical end, will also attend the death of loved ones with the utmost grief because, for him, they are lost and he can henceforth no longer communicate his love to them. The believer, however, knows that the beloved deceased belongs to a new world in which truth attains its full meaning. The deceased no longer needs to be cared for because he has entered into the fullness from which he can care with eternal efficacy for those he has left behind. This ability to be efficacious belongs to the deposit of faith and, thus, to the things that are more essential and efficacious than transient things. The person who has gone home to God has found his ultimate destiny from which he sends crucial things to those who are left behind for the fulfillment of their earthly task.

Perhaps unconsciously, nonbelievers pose the question of God in their search for a meaning to life that will outlive them. They are on their way to faith, even if this is not yet a concept for them. It is, however, impossible to find a self-contained meaning for human life within transience. Nonbelievers basically ask for eternal, divine values without knowing their name. A genuine nonbeliever could therefore only be someone who goes about his business completely in the here and now, someone who finds himself and his surroundings so satisfying and so fit for every kind of perfection that he would obviously lack any sense of the future of life or its transience. He wants and can set no expectations because today is completely sufficient for him. The thinking person, however, goes through time laden with questions; he feels, and should feel, each insight granted to him to be nothing more than a fragment, since time and again it can be continued, supplemented, and interpreted in different ways. This person knows that his reason will never be enough to construct a totally satisfying world view. Even if he were to sketch a world that were sufficient for today, he would nonetheless have to place a question mark after most assertions as a sign of their provisional nature. But when the Son says that he is the truth and that he brings the Word, which he himself is, from eternity, the believer also grasps in light of this Word why all his thoughts, love, and desire to give of himself necessarily stumble into boundaries here below that will be definitively removed only in heaven; he is on his way to God, and his transience is ultimately a sign of this movement.

IV

THE COMMUNICATION
OF TRIUNE LOVE

The believer's view of God's love is determined by the manifestation of the Son. The Son becomes man in order to redeem men for God. The resolve to do this was fixed forever in heaven in the counsel of the Divine Persons. Through the Son, we have a glimpse into this resolve and into the eternal, inner-divine love that now shines forth in each phase of Christ's life as man. He has assumed human exis-tence in order to prove to the Father that his world and his people are good. The Son thus transports the Father back to the days of creation before the judgment that he, the Father, pronounced. The Son's love of the Father's work is an expression of his love of the Father.

We can scarcely conceive a being who would com-pletely transform all its personal conditions of life just to please someone else. This being would, so we think, retain at least its own habits so as not to turn absolutely everything upside down. At certain times it would be of service to its beloved, but at other times it could then return to being itself. The Son, however, has chosen to be not himself. Instead, he has chosen to be a man on earth wholly and completely and to retain only his vision of the Father. He has assumed all the contingencies of our life without distancing himself from the Father's love. Neither in his childhood nor in his hidden years nor in his public life nor on the Cross did he lose hold of the idea at the bottom of it all—the idea of being a man among other men out of love for the Father. This love, which endures unaltered throughout his life and which we can corroborate during his entire earthly life, bears the marks of divine love in its unshakeable steadfastness.

A human life spent in discipleship of Christ can also attain something of this characteristic. When a person sacrifices his life out of love for God, by allowing God to send him out on a given mission or by enduring martyrdom or by allowing himself to be completely diverted from his own plans and intentions, it is love that moves him to do so. This love cannot be equated with the love that people have for one another, which moves them to regular acts of love of neighbor. Rather, this person is so gripped by the God who loves him that his gift of self—however long or short God intends it to be—bears the mark of eternity. Admittedly, anyone who does not love God will never be able to grasp the motivation that inspires such people or the profound effect that divine love has in their life; because what is visible in their life is simply the reflection of their answer to God's love; their existence in their gift of self is the imitation of that which came to the fore uniquely in the life of the Son. A person who has made a gift of self lives entirely out of the love of the Son for the Father. What enables him to lead his life is in no sense of this world. Though the Son has lived in this world, he did so on the strength of his inner-divine love. And when, in bidding farewell to the world he loves, he promises to send his Spirit, he does so on the strength of his knowledge of the Spirit and in order to let his love become all the more efficacious on earth from heaven. The descending Spirit will therefore accomplish in his way the same thing that the Son accomplished living as man: out of the inner-divine love he will administer something that enables man to lay eyes on this love. The Spirit, whose descent transforms men and strengthens them in faith and love, takes over and continues the Son's task. To a certain extent, he does so without a sound and without letting his work appear his own. In all this he is bound to the Son in a way that presents a mirror image of the Son's obedience to the Father. All things lead back to the Father.

But it is not just the manifestation of the Son and of the Spirit that reveals the inner-divine love and its reciprocity between the Divine Persons. Rather, it is each and every *word* of the Son concerning heaven and his being in heaven. He says to the thief: "Truly, I say to you, today you will be with me in Paradise."

In saying this he utters the loftiest promise that can ever be granted to a human being. He promises the apostles that he will drink the new wine with them in the Father's kingdom. These and similar words are filled with a most profound joy; he promises and delivers what belongs to him and to the Father and to the Spirit; the joy expressed relates to the divine togetherness in heaven. It is for this that he redeems human beings in the Father's unending love. Each word that he has spoken would have to be grasped in its unfathomable depths out of his love for the Father and out of inner-divine love in general. Each and every one of these words, which we so often hear scattered all over the place these days, is filled to the brim with divine love; when people profess to be looking for God's love without finding it, they need only pay attention to these words.

Similarly, the Son's *commandment of love*, which extols the love of one person for another as the meaning and goal of life, is nothing other than the expression of inner-divine love. We should love one another because God loves us so much and because God simply is love. And when we are commanded to be as perfect as our heavenly Father is perfect, this is only a completion of the commandment of love, because perfection consists in, and leads to, merciful, eternal love. A love of neighbor that is directed exclusively toward human beings and disregards God's love would ultimately form an egotistical circle; such a love would produce a reciprocal love that corresponded to it but that would be terminated and extinguished in this reciprocity. Man would dissociate himself from his infinite purpose. However, when a believer loves a fellow believer, he loves him in a way directed toward God; he loves his neighbor with a view to God. This is not simply in a love that he can measure or monitor, but in a love that places him in the service of the ever greater God, a love that he offers up like an act of worship so that God might perfect it. He does not just love with his sight directed at human beings, and his love may not just be fruitful in his own sense of it; he entrusts his love to God so that God can draw it to himself and let it be efficacious from heaven. Such love might just as well be called prayer as called love; for God accepts all genuine love like a prayer in order to use it exactly where he needs it. He can make do just as well with the love of two lovers or the love of a believer for his parish and Church or a believer's love of God as he can with an express sacrifice or prayer. He takes this love to himself, sanctifies it completely, and gives it back sanctified to the world, to the Church, and to men in order to lead them back to God.

~

If the Son is the Word of the Father in the beginning, this Word begets love. The Word begets love outwardly in the Incarnation, as human beings experience the triune love through the Son and accept his word as the word of love. However, the Son bears within himself the love, which he outwardly heralds, in his *vision* of the Father. This vision signifies for him the love that unites him with the Father as much on earth as it does in heaven. Whenever he seeks solitude in order to pray, it is evident that he does not speak to the Father in merely formulaic words—even the words that he has taught us—but rather he prays within the vision that for him implies an exchange with the Father. The vision gains the upper hand within him so as to claim all space for the Father, an infinite space corresponding to their mutual love.

The first Christians already knew that they too should withdraw to pray; that they too needed silence in order to put themselves at the disposal of the Father, Son, and Spirit; and, at these times, that they should erase anything that was otherwise preoccupying them so as to be a pure mirror for God. Looking at God—which in the Christian corresponds to the Son's vision—is *contemplation*. Contemplation reaches ahead in two senses. First of all, it is preparation for the eternal vision of the Father in heaven. It is then a laying open of the entire person to receive what God gives him by way of answer in the form of inspirations of the Spirit, insights, or—if God so chooses—genuine visions. The latter belong wholly and completely to contemplation; they are a pre-vision, in which God shows what he wants to show so that not only the person at prayer but also, through him, the Church might be enriched. In a corresponding way, however, prayer is also fulfilled in contemplation. It is not the case that God attends to our supplications straightaway or gives the answers we expect. It is more likely that he gives to the believer absorbed in the Church the answer of love that corresponds best to the Church and to the plans of God. Thus, all contemplation becomes a dialogue of love. And each Gospel mystery that is reflected upon is the expression of this love, regardless of whether it is a miracle or the Cross or a feast at which the Lord takes part or a parable he tells or his entire being as the Son of Man. All contemplation bears fruit that proceeds from it immediately, and this fruit is likewise the answer of love, which will express itself in the believer as an increased love of God, a more profound initiation into his mysteries, or as the taking on of a specific task. If the contemplation is genuine, it will become the departure point for a renewal in the person who prays, a renewal whose depth can scarcely be measured but which, at all events, effects a new gift of self and a new love of God.

In this sense, contemplation is also an answer to

the Father's creation. The Father created the world out of love, and it is an object of his reflection. His purely divine love has created for itself a graspable expression of love. The judgment "very good" at the end of each day of the creation means that his love has found a counterpart in what he has created and can delight in it. His love has proof of its superabundance and has handed out its fruit in the form of the world that has come newly into being. Everything that is the Father's created expression of his love should therefore answer in love. When the Creator sees the boundless sea with its waves or the sky with its immeasurable clouds, he recognizes his creatures in them, indications of his infinity, mirror images that he has given to men in order to make known something of himself by analogy. Many people live in suffocating conditions, oppressed by their fellowmen. In a human atmosphere they often find God only with difficulty; they need to look up and to catch their breath; they need a neutral and less confined medium to remind them of God and to strengthen their tired faith and love. A great landscape restores peace and stillness to them—not a landscape that amounts to nothing more than itself, but one that tells of God's peace, brings his silence close, and hints at his eternal sameness, which is always new and overwhelming for us nonetheless.

There is no boredom in contemplation because contemplation is the answer to the creative love of the Father; in itself it is therefore the love of the creature, and love cannot spoil. The love of the Father for the Son and for the Spirit, together with their answer of love to the Father, are contained in his love for the world. In the same way, an ardent cycle of love should prevail in creaturely contemplation, as men come to know that they are loved by God even when they do not understand it, even when they know themselves to be changeable and, accordingly, recognize God in the various faces and forms of behavior that the Creator wants to show to his creature and that do not simply coincide with each other: the countenance of joy or rest, of severity or mercy, and so forth. These "faces" of God are reflected in the Church, in the sacraments, in the Church's feasts, and in liturgical prayer, which finds its fulfillment whenever it once more paves new paths for loving contemplation.

And in all this God has the world before him as an object of his love. He experiences the love of men as something that he has not simply created but that has poured forth from within him, so that throughout all transient time, proofs of this love will pour back to him as guarantees that created love will remain creative for all eternal time through the sacrifice of the Son.

~

On the Mount of Olives, the Son prays: "My Father, if it be possible, let this cup pass from me." On the Cross he cries: "My God, my God, why hast thou forsaken me." These are words that proclaim his *suffering* at its utmost intensity. Already suffering his suffering in anticipation, the Son sees an opportunity for the cup to pass from him. That the Father nonetheless allows the Cross shows that, from the outset, this has to count as a sign of his paternal love: his love is so great that it permits his Son to give to the farthest extreme. The plan decided upon in heaven is to unfold to its end. And it goes so far that the Son no longer senses the presence of the Father and feels abandoned. The love of the Father for the Son is not limited by what a man can still or can no longer bear. This love lets the Son die on earth so that no measure might be set on heavenly love and it might pour forth freely. Human barriers are forced open. Should a lover want to sacrifice his life for his beloved, she would not accept the sacrifice were she to learn of it. She would believe that she owed it to her love to say no, to let her lover live and rather to die herself. But purely human love presupposes finitude and does not reckon with a boundless gift of self. Even when a martyr gives his life for God, he is not free from all restricting measures: he knows, for instance, the measure of the sin that he does not want to commit and which for him would now be to deny God. Nonetheless, he allows his love to flow into the immeasurability of God's love, a love of which he, like all men, can have only the faintest idea. And his consciousness of the presence of God will hardly abandon him at his death. The Son, however, dies in complete abandonment. He alone enters into the ultimate possible self-gift, and the Father accepts the sacrifice without unveiling himself, because, from the outset, he regards this as befitting his immeasurable divine love.

The Son, who is God, has lived though a genuine earthly fate and made a unique sacrifice to the love of the Father. When, having returned to the Father, the Son sends forth the *Spirit*, the Spirit does not become man and does not live an earthly fate. Vestiges of the Spirit can be ascertained from events like Pentecost and from conversions that he effects; it is possible to tell of and see how he transforms the fate of men; but one cannot attribute a fate of his own to him. Once again this is a sign of the vitality of the inner-divine love: the Son may well send the Spirit as he was sent by the Father, yet this is something independent and not a repetition. For the Spirit will not imitate the Son; rather, he will blow where he will. He will not let himself be caught, defined, or grasped in any form. God will accept men on the basis of the Son's sacrifice and recognize in individual believers the sign of the Son who has suffered for all. However, the Father, together with the Son, will recognize Christians in whom the Spirit has taken effect. He works in those whom the Son has marked; for it belongs to the Son to imprint the ecclesial sign of belonging. Nor does the Spirit let himself be seen in human form; rather, he lets himself be seen in other forms that are all symbolic. Much can be gathered about the infinity of God's love—a love that shows so many different characteristics—from the difference between the workings of the Son and those of the Spirit.

Were we to apply this to the believer, we would learn that though we allow ourselves to be influenced by people and we can live from their faith, we can only do so until the moment in which we have to transform on our own; for we have to imitate the Son and not the spirit of the individual as such. For if the spirit of the individual is guided by the Holy Spirit, it points to the Son and, by means of this pointer, shares in the Son's task of being the door to the Father.

V

THE HOLY SPIRIT AND
HOW HE PAVES THE WAY
TO THE FATHER

The apostles were together at Pentecost. They saw
the Spirit descend upon them in tongues of fire and
experienced him in the miracle of tongues. This experience was twofold. First, it was external, unusual,
and incomparable with anything they knew, possibly
terrifying and its meaning uninterpretable. Second,
it was an inner disclosure of new capabilities that
surpassed their usual habits and the strength of their
intellect. Both dimensions of the experience were
the sign of the arrival of the divine Spirit, and both
became fully intelligible for the first time in their
being a sign. The sudden expansion of the apostles'
powers of speech, which came into effect straightaway, proved that they were being acquainted with
a new world without the merit, learning, or practice
of their own eyes or linguistic skill. But this explo-
sion of the apostles' capabilities also meant gathering them together insofar as the same thing befell
them all and they could reassure one another of it.
The first thing that this gathering together brought
about was a common testimony: in every language

they testified to the same thing. But because this testimony was about the divine Spirit whom the Son had promised to send, the event had to go far beyond a testimony to an earthly happening. Torn beyond their former boundaries, they were transported, from above, into the reality that the Son had promised and now bestowed. In this reality they not only experienced the existence of the Spirit but also experienced his relation to the Son who sends him and to the Father who sends the Son. This insight implies a living faith in the Spirit; faith, not within its former historical and human limits, but within something completely new that was both a confirmation of all that had been and an infinite expansion. The divine Spirit was therefore capable of assuming a face; moreover, he was capable of transforming the apostles, of elevating them way beyond their own measure and capabilities and enabling them to participate in an unforeseen world—the world of God. But this expansion was at the same time their Yes to everything that had come before, for it was the fulfillment of it. It was the fulfillment of the Son's promise, the fulfillment of their faith in the Son, who from heaven gave them the signal for his arrival at the right hand of the Father, the sign of his efficacy, of his living remembrance of the world and of his eternal life together with the Father and the Spirit.

It is difficult to form a concrete image of the perfection of the *Father* in the New Testament because when the Son becomes man, he withdraws, so to speak, and leaves the entire revelation to the Son. In the Old Testament, the Father was the one who acted and spoke, but he had promised the Jews that he would send his Messiah. When the prophets prophesied, they did so in the name of the Father; where some heard his voice, others saw deeds and signs that they had to assume, in faith, came from the Father; others experienced things in their visions that were suited to preparing them for the New Testament and to expanding their faith in God. With hindsight, we can say that the place of the Holy Spirit already becomes visible in this paternal revelation— for much in revelation has to be described as nothing less than the immediate "voice of the Father" —and yet it expressed the Father's wish and decree and was, therefore, the Spirit of the Father and was meant to be a mediation leading men to the Son.

When the Son says in the New Testament, "You, therefore, must be perfect, as your heavenly Father is perfect", there is only one thing necessary to form an image of the Father's perfection: seeing the *Son* live. But because he lives entirely as a man, it is not easy to distinguish between the human and the divine in him. In his earthly life he realizes such a perfect unity of them both that for as long as we just look at the Father through the Son, we see him only in about the same way as a one-eyed person sees a landscape. The image acquires relief and perspective by taking the *Holy Spirit* into account. We now look to the Father through the Son and the Spirit, who are both God. It is like looking into a stereoscope in which there are two images that are imperceptibly different from one another; we see only *one* image, an image that now acquires vividness and depth. By means of the three-dimensionality that the Spirit brings to the image of God, we experience a lot about the Father but also about the Son, about the Spirit himself, and about the whole trinitarian God.

The Spirit shows himself in manifold characteristics, workings, and powers, which would perhaps seem dry and theoretical to us and, together, represent only an abstract supreme being were he not himself at the same time the living, personal Spirit of the Father and of the Son. It is therefore precisely through the apparent abstractness of the Spirit that the complete inner-divine life becomes concrete. For the Father wants our faith itself to become trinitarian and alive through the manifestation of the Son and the sending forth of the Spirit. He does not want our faith in the Trinity of God to remain two-dimensional and theoretical, nor does he want us to see the one Person only when, and to the extent that, he presents himself, almost as if he were an object contemplated from a distance. Instead, we should be able to perceive each Person revealing himself in his unity with the others and, consequently, in their infinite, divine breadth. This unity, however, is the expression of love.

If we want a human image for this, we can start with human love: with two people in love with one another and who no longer want to be understood in their own right. When a third party attempts to understand one of them, they explain that neither they nor their lives can be considered in their own right; rather they can only be appreciated if the one they love is understood; without the one they love, each of them is robbed of his life, his achievements, his home, his very where and what; everything about them obtains its validity from love alone; without love, any image or picture of them becomes distorted. The same is equally true of them both: they cannot be taken fully as themselves without the other; anything they represent on their own lacks truth and life if it is not appreciated as the expression of their love. They lose their freedom and their joy in being if someone tries to understand them in an image defined individually. On their own, each would resemble someone who had had his photograph taken in a glorious landscape. If the landscape were artificially removed from the photograph, all that would be left would be a lone figure who would not be the person he was when the photograph was taken. No one, not even the person in the photograph, would anymore be able to say when and where the photograph had been taken. If reminded of the moment, he would say that he had felt himself to be in the landscape and wanted to be tied closely to it, together with all the things that then constituted his life and that he wished to preserve in his memory.

If the Spirit is the exchange of love of the Father and of the Son, the Father thus wants to see him and the Son, and also wants to know that they are seen, so that his picture will be complete. The Son and the Spirit are, in an analogous sense, his landscape and life's breath. Thus, when the Son says, "You, therefore, must be perfect, as your heavenly Father is perfect" or "Thy will be done, on earth as it is in heaven", the image of the Father that is presupposed is only completed and strengthened by sending the Spirit. For the Spirit, even though he is sent to us by the Son, comes from the Father and returns to him in a similar movement to that of the Son, whose goal is to draw us closer to the Father. And because we are always in danger of misinterpreting the visibleness of the Son and overlooking that which is divine in him because of that which is human, the Spirit appears in a form that cannot be apprehended. The fact that he is just spirit also deepens our image of the Son and prevents a one-sided anthropomorphization of the Son. The task of the Spirit is to proclaim the Father and the Son, and he carries out this task by leading us into a deeper understanding of God that is bound to a greater faith. However, this greater faith shows itself as our will to make a more complete gift of self, as our will to trust more unceasingly. And deeper understanding is a better insight into the images that point to God and into their application. On the basis of both, however, the Spirit can seize us in an even more profound way. In the areas in which we tend to fail, he has as his goal new successes that will draw us closer to the Father and the Son, that will set in motion whatever is immovable within us, that will bend whatever is stiff and transform us so completely that we no longer recognize ourselves or need to recognize ourselves, for the recognition demanded of us now lies in God.

∼

At Confirmation, the believer receives the Holy Spirit in a form that is at once ecclesial and paternal. It is ecclesial insofar as it is sacramental and paternal, because the Holy Spirit opens up the spirit of the believer to the Father. When a little child begins to understand religious images and his mother tells him stories about the baby Jesus and the Mother of God or stories from the Old Testament, each of the figures takes on its own shape in his childlike spirit. The baby Jesus is a child like other children, but one who does nothing naughty and can lead other children to be as good as he is. It is similar with the other figures. Everything that is imagined remains immediate and uncomplicated. This corresponds to the world of the child. The child playing on the beach absorbs thousands of individual impressions: here is the pile of sand with which the child is playing; there are the waves in which he splashes; out there are the ships sailing on the sea. The child can gather childlike experiences about the ebb and flow of the tide, can see the water rise and the rocks being submerged by it. When the child is bigger he learns to contemplate the sun setting over the ocean and to look in amazement at the expanse of the horizon. But the child needs the maturity of being grown up in order to encounter the total phenomenon of the sea, its mighty impact extending farther than the eye can see, the hidden world of its depths that impedes explorers time and again; indeed, all the mysterious things about the ocean that cannot be reduced to any one formula.

Something similar happens with the bestowal of the Holy Spirit in Confirmation: the unrelated images of Christian life up until then are gathered to the Father; but as soon as the concepts cease to be mere names in our human world of relations, the mystery of the Father begins to become evident in our spirit, proclaimed through the Holy Spirit and apprehensible only through him. No boundaries have been set to his introduction of the human spirit to the mysteries of the Father. Considered in this way, Confirmation is the believer's being received into God's wholly supernatural world of mystery, which can no longer be apprehended through human analogies; Confirmation is the initiation into the above and beyond that exceeds any natural image of the world; it is the definitive insight that everything that we know about the Father and can enunciate is infinitely different and greater in him. For the believer, this insight means an invitation to believe more profoundly, not merely to be on the lookout for new objects of faith, but rather to perceive in what is apprehended that which cannot be apprehended.

However, the sacramentally efficacious Spirit whom the Son has sent also mediates the valid image of the Church. When the Church mediates the Spirit, she gives what has been able to give her the form the Son meant her to have. When she administers the sacrament of Confirmation, the Church enriches herself in the sense of a greater obedience to the Son and to the Father. Through the Spirit, the Church becomes the chief representation of trinitarian love in the world.

The Spirit is sent by the Son, but only after the Son's return to the Father. The fact that the Father and Son are together is therefore decisive in the sending forth of the Spirit. That the Spirit is sent is proper to the return of the Son's completed mission to the Father. His arrival at the right hand of the Father is the seal on the Son's mission and the expression of its acceptance by the Father: it is the sign of the completion of the triune love that is presenting itself in the world. The sacrament of Confirmation is therefore a special expression of this united love in the simultaneously highest possible differentiation of the Persons who are revealing themselves. The love of God is communicated so that the faithful are made able to love God out of the same love. It is perfect integrity because it is perfect, selfless love. Just as the Son came to reveal, not himself, but the Father, so too is the Spirit sent, not to show himself or to act in his own name, but rather to represent the Father in the name of the Son in a new way so that the love that is in God might also be in us.

VI

THE SON'S BOUNDEDNESS AND BOUNDLESSNESS

The Son rests in the Father throughout the Old Testament. There are prophecies that proclaim his coming and, moreover, speak in a mysterious way of his existence in heaven with the self-revealing God and with the equally mysterious Spirit of God. The hour in which the Son will come to the fore has not yet come. In the fullness of time, the Son appears as a little human child; but his divinity is made known when the angel appears to Mary and when the star appears to the three kings. Mary's virginity is required to elevate the Son's becoming man above the beginning of life of all other men; the star is used in order to show that the Creator stands in a special relationship to this particular child and that the heavens are willing to bend their rules to the needs of the Son. For the kings, the star is not just something supernatural that stimulates their faith; rather, it is something terrifying that exceeds all the expectations of human calculation and forces them into a genuflection of mind and spirit. From that time on, their correct path lies in being led by the star, which makes known to them the superior might of heaven.

They follow. They learn an obedience about which they hitherto knew not a thing. It is quite the opposite of blind obedience: it is a seeing obedience; it is an obedience that is already sight (indeed, they are constantly looking at the star), but it is a sight that leads to real sight—into the vision of the Son.

This sight has something almost visionary about it: the child is unprepossessing, lying in a stall and cradled in poverty; the kings' gifts are the first things to break through this poverty and ordinariness. Considered without faith, the scene would remain incomprehensible: the rich men seem to give the poor child mere things that he does not need in an abundance that is inappropriate given his situation and with an awe that no king will ever show to a human child. The gravity of their kingly might and richness is thus lost in the sight of the child: they stand as good as disempowered before the superior might of God; their genuflection becomes the conversion of all human relations. Their faith becomes the renunciation of all that is theirs, which they lay at the feet of the child.

The supernatural, which accompanies the manifestation of the child, has shown itself in the form that God wanted. The position that the child holds amid the angels, the stars, and the gifts is that of an emptiness amid magnificence; it is the cessation of kingly splendor and the extinguishment of the light of the star. In the place of vision comes faith, the faith of those who have vision, and the vision is completely transferred onto the Son, who has the vision of the Father, but without the men who now have faith gaining any inkling of the Son's beatific vision. This is a consequence of an exchange: the unprepossessing nature of the child appears as the invisible, naked divine nature, yet not as that of the child himself, but as the being of the Father in the child, as the Father's self-extinguishment in the Son who is becoming manifest; for the Son, however, this means a new vision of the Father. His vision is now that of one who has become man and sees the Father in heaven—he does not merely see the "open heavens", but he truly sees the Father; he does not simply have a certain inkling of what is happening in the eternal heavens; rather, he contemplates this life as one who comes from the life of heaven.

But the Son wants to be completely human and to acquire for himself the spiritual posture that seems best for his disciples in order, not only to be the Son of God on earth, but to be a son of man in all things. Within his vision of God there is a complete unfolding that ends on the Cross as he cries out, "My God, my God, why hast thou forsaken me?" Of course, this unfolding is to be interpreted, not as a human, natural development, but rather as a consequence of the circumstances in which the Son wants to live in order that his sacrifice might be completed in absolute abandonment. Everything that exists en route between his vision and his abandonment will win from him the form that his disciples will call Christian faith.[1] Each of Christ's disciples will have to maneuver at the midpoint between vision and abandonment. This midpoint will, of course, appear in different ways at different times, but in all its variations it will be genuine Christian faith—provided that it springs from that which the Son experienced between his birth and death as man.

Everything that a believer does, thinks, and undertakes in his daily life, and everything that seems proper to his life on earth, is nonetheless done always in faith, that is, in the knowledge that God sees it and that the sum of the believer's actions constitute a Christian existence. The believer cannot suddenly desert his faith to pursue things that are completely outside the rules of faith; he cannot shape his life as if God did not exist with the thought that the same could also be done if God did exist and could be justified both before faithless reason and before the supernatural God and approved of as much by God as by faithless men. He therefore has to decide on one attitude—the attitude of faith. It is on one

[1] This sentence is key to what follows. Christ does not have Christian faith because he has the vision of the Father, which ultimately assumes the form of night and abandonment; but Christian faith originates—as is self-evident—immediately from Christ's attitude and example, from his conformity to the situation of mankind. Hence Paul calls him "the pioneer and perfecter of our faith" (Heb 12:2).—ED.

attitude, however, that the Son, too, is constantly deciding by constantly doing the will of the Father and using the merest human acts to fulfill his Father's will. And this divine-human posture of obedience, born of freedom, is the fundamental source of the Christian faith. Certain mystics, like Saint John of the Cross, have given us precise depictions, on the one hand, of what their "abandonment" in the spiritual night was like and, on the other hand, of how their "vision" of God looked. We know that both night and vision were carried, accompanied by, and born of Christian faith. In the life of the Son it works the other way around: out of the extremes of vision and abandonment he lets something come into being in his life that earns the name of faith when it is translated into the form of Christian discipleship. This happens under the influence of the Holy Spirit, who is constantly cooperating in the life of the Son.

This is already recognizable in the Son's Incarnation. Throughout his life, the Son will dwell in the threefold relationships that were already foreshadowed in the threefold relationships of Mary's conception. As one who believes and makes a gift of herself, Mary is given the vision of the heavenly angel. In the vision of the Annunciation she experiences the descent of the Holy Spirit. And when the Son becomes man—sent by the Father and carried and accompanied into the Mother's womb by the Spirit—he reveals in this becoming what sort of being he will have on earth: an existence of mission through the Father, accompanied by the Spirit, coming from the vision, proceeding into abandonment, with a dynamic center that, when transferred to those who follow him, can become the spiritual attitude of faith.

The Christian faith, insofar as it has its archetype in the Son, is therefore not principally an issue of doctrine—for example, about the Persons in God —formulated on the basis of a position of distance toward God that would turn him into a mere object of thought. The relationship of the incarnate Son to the Father and to the Spirit has nothing abstract about it and does not cease to be for the Son what it was for all eternity in heaven—his living, spiritual life. But from now on, it is conformed to human nature, which, insofar as it is the nature of the eternal Son, forever has the vision of the Father but, insofar as it is the same nature as that of all other men, translates this experience of God into a form that is bearable in our situation. In the complete experience of Christian doctrine that he both brings and *is*, the Son brings to men—not just in his name, but equally in the name of the Father and of the Spirit —that which he brought from heaven as he became man and which on earth he lets become an earthly, human experience. It would be completely perverse to limit the Incarnation to the Son's merely robing

himself with a body; the Son is essentially the redeeming man for all because he bears away the sins
of all in his soul and because, in doing so, he also gar-
ners human experiences so as to give them to men
anew, transformed by him and as his very own. He
keeps the vision of the Father to himself, as the Father has instructed him. He also keeps the ultimate
abandonment on the Cross to himself, and that, too,
is obedience to the Father. However, what he gives
to men between birth and death is his divine-human
experience of God, which is communicated to us according to our human measure and in us becomes
faith.

When a Christian tries to lead someone to faith,
he shows him the truths of faith. If this Christian
is a mystic, he will not tell his non-Christian friend
about his visions as a way of bringing him to faith
more quickly. The non-Christian may feel that his
teacher possesses experiences of faith of which he
—so long as he does not know how to pray and
is not blessed in the same way—can have scarcely
any idea. The teacher will mediate general truths
of faith, admittedly not without connections to his
own experience of faith; he will mediate doctrine,
not as something abstract that has been assimilated
from books, but rather in an experiential form of
his faith directed at specific concrete realities within
the ecclesial realm. Thus, the Son, too, on earth has
an experiential form of that which he is to mediate

to his disciples as Christian faith. The truth that he
brings to us is connected profoundly to what he experiences as the God-Man as well as to what goes
into the crafted words and ideas with which he communicates this truth to us. He does not say, "See the
Father as I see him"; he invents parables and expres-
sions in the Holy Spirit that speak in a human way
and can affect the human spirit. But he does not do
that just externally by remaining within his vision
for his own sake and dispatching from there merely
his word to those who do not have the vision. As the
living Word of God, he *himself* goes each and every
time into the experience of those who do not have
the vision. And he does this, not because he wants
to pose as man before our eyes or wants to demon-
strate to us that he is a human being, but rather because he *is* a man in all simplicity and truth.

God the Father, with the Son and with the Spirit,
is so infinite that there are no limits to this infinity. Rather, he was able to create an appropriate expression of his infinity in the Son's descent into the
finitude of human life. Given to us men by the Son,
this expression of God's infinity is faith.

～

In the course of the Old Testament, the Jews received an idea of the Father that, on the one hand,
already lay in the creation while, on the other, was

determined by God's interventions in the destiny of the people, by the voice of the prophets, by the promises, and, finally, to a strong degree by the people's sin and by their turning away. Throughout all this, God and man stood facing one another at a distance that permitted no ultimate intimacy, because man was no longer in his original state of being turned toward God but rather had to be called back repeatedly from his state of being turned away from God. He was unable correctly to grasp the image that God wanted to show him because he could not look at or see it correctly. The Son, however, is the man who looks and sees, the man who has the vision. He lives in this vision, in this looking toward and seeing the Father. What his disciples have to learn from his vision is to remain turned toward God, to conform themselves to God's will. And this attitude is, not forced, but rather assumed in the freedom of love. The Son, who sees the Father and is obedient to him unto death, is not able to do otherwise because divine love cannot do otherwise. This is not, however, a love that cloaks itself in baffling mysteries; rather, it is a love unveiled in the Son. The Son sees the Father and thereby reveals him.

Men thus receive the Son in Christian teaching as the example of the correct attitude to assume. When the Father spoke with the first human beings in Paradise, they stood facing him as creatures who were more in awe of him than in love with him. After their turning away, God no longer showed himself as himself; he let his voice be heard and gave instructions and commandments; men could not claim that God had left them on their own but had to concede that sin alone had created the distance between them. Men had to look through their guilt to God; in the best case this could lead to them becoming watchful but not to a glimpse or a spiritual vision of God. Man had become like one who strains his eyes in order to see a picture that is not sufficiently illuminated.

In the New Testament, the believer knows that the Son sees the Father. However, the Son mediates, not his vision, but something that is derived from it—faith. Faith is like a shaft of light that leads to God. This light reaches the believer, not unbroken, but rather through the prism of Christian doctrine. What the Father gives to us has the form of vision for the Son, but it has the form of faith for us because it requires mediation through the Son who says, "No one comes to the Father but by me." And Christian doctrine is the word of the Son given to men. In the bosom of the Father, Son and Word are one. But when the Son lives among us as man, it is possible to distinguish two aspects of his reality: he is a living man with flesh and blood, the messenger of the Father, and his teaching is the epitome of the message he brings.

So that the Son and his teaching can remain living among us, the Lord establishes the Church. He creates the Church for himself as his bride, which therefore keeps him, the Bridegroom, "in her vision". The Church is a mysterious, living, and spiritual reality. She is not, however, a creaturely person. Were she such a person, she would dwell in the permanent vision of the Bridegroom subjectively as well; however, as an institution, it is objectively that she stands before him. The expression for this objective relationship of the Church to the Lord is the ecclesial office; in this way, the Church's vision of her Lord is meant to be universally valid. Everything that bears the character of subjective vision in the individual believer must necessarily bow to the ecclesial norm. The Son therefore mediates his vision in a twofold way: he gives to the office an objective "vision" that, as such, cannot be realized subjectively; and he gives to individuals a vision that takes effect in a subjective-objective way but that must be affirmed in the sight of the Church, just as our entire Christian faith is affirmed to the highest degree through the Son's gaze directed toward the Father.

When the Son founds the Church, he reveals, no longer just himself, but himself and the Church in their relationship as bridegroom and bride. This I-You relationship is one created for the world in order to reflect, in a form suited to faith, the I-You relationship between Father and Son. If the Son has come to reveal the Father, the Church exists in order to reveal the Son. The Church has to be an expression of the Son's will, just as the Son is the expression of the Father's will. But both are eternal divine love—both the will of the Father and the Son as an expression of this will; and so the Church, too, is a representation of this same love. While the individual believer leads a transient human life, the Son fashions a house beyond this transience that is intended for the duration of the world—the Church, which as such is a reflection of eternity and holds transient life within herself, as the one that she is and as a community. When an isolated individual is received into the Church, he is placed in the communion of saints at a fixed point, at a place determined personally by God that is, at the same time, a place of community.

The revelation of the Father through the Son now receives a new face once more. Through the founding of the Church, the Son reveals the Father to the individual but also to the community. The Father allows himself to be revealed, through the One who is the Son, to the one that is the Church and is communion. The redemption through the death of the Son on the Cross is mediated to the many by this one Church. This is bound, not just to the Person of the Son alone, but also to his life revealing the Father in the Spirit. The Church is therefore bound immediately to the Father by the mediator; and the faithful find the Father whom the Son reveals through the Church that reveals herself in the Son.

～

The Father has always revealed himself: from eternity to the Son in the Spirit; in a new way by becoming Creator; and, eventually, in a form that lies somewhere between the creation out of chaos and the Incarnation of God, that is, in the first man. Adam is created in accordance with God's archetype, as an image from and to the archetype, who is God. But Adam is also created according to the Son, to the extent that the Son, as the second Adam, will be the vessel for God and will become man as God—man in the form of the first Adam. These are all revelations of the Father in which he makes known his will. Having disregarded this will by sinning, man is no longer able to recognize the expression of God's pure love in creation, and for this reason, the Father ultimately reveals himself in the Son who is love; for he knows that the Son will never relinquish this love and will never disappoint him; he knows that no man will ever be able to see anything in the Son other than the revelation of the Father's love. It is a reciprocal revelation: the Father reveals himself actively in the Son, while the Son actively reveals the Father. It is the exuberant restoration of the reciprocity that existed between the Creator and Adam but was spoiled by sin. This reciprocity no longer has its initial static form, which from the start was always prone to inertia, but instead has a dynamic openness that makes space for all the vitality desired by God. This active vitality between the Father and the Son becomes apparent through the Spirit, that is to say, this relationship has space for the variety that the Spirit brings about in faithful humanity. This dynamic is something neither fuzzy nor chaotic: it has the strength and form of genuine life. And because God's life is love, this space is a space that leads the faithful into love.

All divine revelation proceeds from and to love. At any place where love might not yet be, God's love presupposes it, in order to awaken the potential love into reality. The man, however, whom the Father reveals is Christ. He has (to our eyes) stepped forth from boundlessness in order to stand out on earth as a figure whom we can follow. By taking upon himself the events of everyday human life and living them in episodes that can be made into narratable actions, which are always comprehensible somewhere or other, he imposes boundaries on himself that originate within our boundedness. We can place the words he has spoken in our own mouths; likewise, we can tread a footpath that he has trodden. But we simply cannot do it with the perfection that is his. Our faith, too, always has boundaries. In the best case, we can perform a series of acts, each of which remains incomplete because our imitation lacks the breath of God, that complete, boundless thing that the Son was able to bring with him from the treasury of the triune life and insert into acts of his boundedness so that the Father might recognize eternal love in them. A person could die a martyr's death in faith for Christ; indeed, he could die on a cross in imitation of Christ's death; he could also form all sorts of affinities to Christ's fundamental attitude in his own interior attitude of sacrifice. In doing so he might surpass earthly boundaries by borrowing from the realm of the supernatural. Faith would give him the confidence that his sacrifice might be fruitful and useful within the sacrifice of Christ; he could suffer through everything with an undaunted Yes that exceeded human strength and stemmed completely from the strength of the Son's Passion. Nonetheless he would have to be aware at the same time that, in all the Christian ever-greater nature of his sacrifice (with regard to Christ's sacrifice), Christ's sacrifice inhabits his own to an infinitely and incomparably greater degree, and Christ's participation in his sacrifice outdoes his participation in Christ's sacrifice by an eternal measure. Ultimately, therefore, the

infinity of God in Christ must come to the aid of
his own finitude.

That would be the highest measure that a Christian could reach. But there is something of it alive
in regular Christian life as well: the knowledge of
a mystery of participation that shifts, indeed, fundamentally transcends, the boundaries of the human in
general, and the boundaries of faith above and beyond that; a participation in what to us is the unfathomable, barely imaginable infinity of the Son, in
which God's eternity and boundlessness is presence.
The Christian can say nothing more about this participation; he knows that it exists; and that is Christian consolation.

In revealing the Father, the Son says, "He who sees
me sees [the Father]." But he also says, "No one
comes to the Father but by me." Thus the Father's
position shifts: in the first passage the Father is in
the Son; in the second he stands behind the Son who
is the door to the Father. And so it seems as if the
Father has distanced himself. The final revelation of
the Son in his earthly life is his cry of abandonment
on the Cross. He now reveals a Father who is no
longer there at all and who has left him all alone. It
is no longer the Father of whom he has the vision,
no longer the Father whom he knows: it is the Father whom he does *not* know and whom he wants

to reveal. It is the revelation of the Father in his absence.[2] The revelation of the Son is such that it not only includes presence but also exceeds presence because it is so truly presence that it no longer comes out as presence. For it is now that the infinity of the Father becomes really visible in this abandonment. The Father has, as it were, disappeared to the end of eternity, though this end can be nothing other than the beginning: that beginning in which there is the Word that is begotten precisely of the Father; and the Father is nowhere else but in this generation of the Word. The Father is completely in the Son. And yet the Son would now have to say that anyone seeing him was *not* seeing the Father. As man, he has been abandoned completely by the Father; as God, however, he is identical with the divinity of the Father. He no longer says, "Not my will, but thine, be done." For the will of the Father has become everything in the Son.

Earlier the subject of discussion was Christ's finitude, which participated in the vision of the Father and in the infinity of his essence. We now reach the ultimate intensification of this: the opening up, not only of finite concepts, but also of the finitude

[2] In the mystery of the Cross, the "absence" of the Father is the mode of suffering (*Leidens-Modus*) of his presence. All transformations spoken of here happen on the basis of changes in Christ's human nature.—Ed.

of Christ in his death, the entry of his infinity on earth into the infinity of the Father in heaven. This is boundless revelation; this is revelation in a purely objective state, in essence, and in the nakedness that in one single second is eternity.

VII

THE FATHER REVEALED
IN THE CHURCH

The believer can glimpse a revelation of the Father
in all the prophecies of the Old Testament, indeed,
in every word that comes from heaven and is accepted on earth. This revelation—as the believer
knows from the perspective of the promise—weighs
more than he suspects, not only on earth, but also
in heaven, and conceals a fullness of divine life that
could never be exhausted in the solitariness of a single person. At the creation, God stepped forth as
the one who separated, ordered, and produced. This
stepping forth did not in any sense represent the end
of an eternal solitariness that had come before it and
had now finally found its partner in man. Rather, it
was a dawning from the heart of the fulfilled divine
life—from it and back to it.

However, the Father—as the Creator and as the
one who speaks from heaven—receives an entirely
new profile through the Incarnation of the Son. The
Son comes in order to proclaim the Father, from
which it can be ascertained that the Father was already revealing the Son and the Spirit in the Old
Testament in a veiled form that was awaiting the

coming of the Son before being unveiled. This latency was aimed at meanwhile placing man before the countenance of his Creator in a relationship that included them both in their entirety: both Creator and creature, both Father and child. When the Son becomes manifest in order to reveal the Father's love, he brings something into the world that had hitherto remained completely veiled: the inner relationship of the triune God in heaven. Sinners had no eye for this. They had accustomed themselves to their state of sin and found all manner of ways to entrench themselves in it. Their joys were like anesthetics against the acute pain of guilt, which could be felt more strongly or more weakly according to the state of the individual sinner's soul. In all this, man believed he could live in a relationship with God in which sin remained a codetermining reality. The Father consequently showed him his justice— the severity of the judge with respect to the sinner. But the fear that man felt at this was not profound enough to keep him from sin. Fear would have had to assume the form of awe and become a transition into love. But this passage was forged only with the coming of the Son.

In the Son, God opens up the heavenly closed circle between Father, Son, and Spirit; he gives the Son to the world, the Son who guarantees the world insight into, and participation in, the life of God. The Son is not an advance guard that has been sent on ahead, nor is the Father the rearguard that will come later. Indeed, the Father presented himself first in the Old Testament, together with the Son and Spirit who were still hidden, and with the promise that everything that had in the meantime not been presented would become evident in its own time. There was a good deal in the promises of the prophets and in the images they saw, which are ultimately affirmed in the images of the Apocalypse, that pointed ahead to the vitality and community of heaven.

God is present for Elijah, not in the storm, but in the still small voice; he shows himself in such gentleness that it remains incomprehensible to man and is only explained when the Father comes to man as the one who exists together with the Son and the Spirit. He adopts the Son's gentleness and the quietness of the Spirit in order to present himself to the prophet; and this communication of his characteristics conveys a hint of an infinite, reciprocal love in which everything appears mutual and exchangeable. When the Father draws close in this form, it already brings close the Son and the Spirit in a way that is supposed to soothe humanity but not to shock it.

When it is said that the Son was the Word in the beginning, this means that, not just the Old Testament, but the whole of creation that existed before it—indeed the whole of eternity—was a communion between Father and Son. The words of the Old Testament thus acquire a new meaning for the believer in the New Testament: a meaning that extends into the triune being of God. The believer now knows that whenever God the Father makes himself known, his eternal Word speaks and hears with him from the beginning. One of the functions of the Word is hearing. The Word sees and hears and feels and experiences this when God communicates with man in Paradise and expels him after the fall. In men, functions are distinguished according to the specific senses. In God, who is all, the Word speaks just as much as he hears and sees. In the beginning, the Creator orders the chaos with regard to man, who is to become his image and likeness. God himself has borne the chaos until the moment in which man is supposed to come into being; for man would not be capable of enduring what is undivided and unseparated. For this reason God furnishes him with distinct abilities—seeing, hearing, speaking—all of which have their archetype in the undivided unity of God. God's Word hears as a whole; man will—in distinction from other creatures—also hear and, in addition, needs the separation and ordering of the world and the course of days. He needs transience and things that can be counted because he himself is one who is counted, because God sets him down as one whom God can count. Even the hairs on his head are counted. But God has never "distinguished" and never counted himself. God never presented himself just as Father to the exclusion of

Son and Spirit, neither when he revealed himself in Paradise nor thereafter. He has opened up his entire divine life. Man alone—who so swiftly grabbed at sin and thus in his own separated senses and functions became incapable of grasping God's indivisibility—has comprehended this revelation of God as something one-dimensional and uni-personal. Only once the love of God, which is indivisible and never counts, reveals itself in the Son will man for the first time be in a position to countenance God's triune being and to count to three in God.

There is no counting in heaven; God is one with the Son and the Spirit; it is we who have to count in order to grasp the truth and fullness of the divine oneness; we, who were created to be counted counters. It is an invention of the Son's love that makes him present the Father and the Spirit to us in differentiation from him—the one who became man—in order to build us a bridge out of our worldly, countable being into that which is divinely uncountable.

∼

Whenever a person tries to determine his situation in the world and in existence, he does so in time. He thinks of the era in which his life takes place and how the years will be divided within that era; he also sees himself between generations that are passing and generations that will come. If he comes from a regular background, he may well be unable to trace his family history back farther than his grandparents. If he comes from a well-known family, he will often know a little more about his ancestors, albeit only through study. He knows the coming generations as his children and grandchildren, and, to a certain extent, he lays the future in their hands; he asks himself what the future might bring them and how they will manage their lives. And just as today he is the grandchild of forebears whom he remembers, so too will he (provided his memory lives on) be the forebear whom his children's children will talk about in just a few decades. Unless some deed or other happens to make him famous, he knows that his name will one day be completely forgotten, and soon (though not if graveyards continue to have such a short life expectancy of their own!) someone will point to his grave and say, "Who was he?"

The Father in heaven remains the Father forever; Father of the whole of humanity, Father of the Son who, together with the Son, brings forth the Spirit who blows where he will. The Father, too, can determine his own course within his eternal time and with regard to creation and his relationship with the Son and with the Spirit. But, unlike a man who conceived his children a long time ago, he is not now merely called a father: his very being is paternal. For all eternity, the Son will call him nothing other than

Father, and he therewith expresses something that is equally true forever, something that is worthy of all awe and praise. Nor will the Spirit ever confuse him with someone or something else, because the Spirit proceeds eternally from him and from the Son and recognizes eternally in him the Father of the Son. This eternal fatherhood is the first thing that God wants to make known about himself to creation; the Father, so to speak, exposes himself first (while as yet keeping the Son and the Spirit behind him) in order first to make clear his relationship to the world and to heaven without there being the possibility of any confusion. All the while, he abides in the eternal exchange of love with the Son, stirred by the Spirit, in a movement that does not stiffen or tire and, therefore, can never stiffen out of habit or boredom for the inhabitants of his heaven who see him. For if we transient beings already have true life, how much more must this be true of the eternal Father! He is so alive that his vivacity surpasses all imagination because it moves in the divine; what we experience of this in faith is scarcely a fragment of the actual reality. And even though we are created according to the image of this divine life (and some day want to be done completely with sin and death), we are, nonetheless, just tiny images that come into being in the midst of transient time and possess limited powers of understanding.

But we have among us the Son who brings us

tidings from the Father. Inevitably, we can sense a relation to the eternal Father in all the words that he directs at us, whether or not he is speaking expressly of the Father. From these words we recognize that the Father is just like the Son, that the Son's ideas are the same as the divine, paternal ideas, that the Father makes a gift of himself just as the Son does, and that this self-gift moreover belongs to the Father's eternal, unchanging essence. In order to love the Son, the Father does not become something other than he is in himself. This love is not accidental; rather he affirms himself by affirming the Son. Father and Son mutually affirm one another, and it is the Spirit in whom and through whom this mutuality is fulfilled and who is himself thereby affirmed.

This triune affirmation implies another affirmation, that is, the affirmation of the Father's work —the affirmation of creation. And men are encouraged, from the outset, not only to cooperate in carrying out God's Yes to the world, but also to allow themselves to be affirmed by him. The "very good" that God says to the world belongs to the "very good" that the Divine Persons say to each other and that expresses each Person in his distinctness from the others. The world finds its place within this relational space. Thus, all that is manifold, countable, and created stands before God, not as something distant from and lesser than him, but as something affirmed by him in his original Yes. And the manifold concepts that the Son uses in order to open up God's world to us are not alien to God in their fullness and reach; rather, they are reflections of eternal import.

When transferred to man, it is God's eternal differentiated being that puts the faithful onto firm, eternal ground. A Christian father is not just a father in the mere passing sense of successive generations. Within the Church, he is related to the fatherhood of the heavenly Father: it is as a believer that he is to be the father of his children. But this relationship—like all others (motherhood, childhood, friendship)—is mediated to men by God through the Church. Because the Holy Spirit is the permanent mediator of the relationships between Father and Son, the Son has fashioned his Church in the Spirit (it is in her that the Father desires to elevate his creation into eternity), and while this bride of the Son becomes the father and mother of the faithful through the Spirit and from God, she mediates supernatural fatherhood and motherhood to the faithful, so long as they are alive in faith, in accordance with the Lord's words: "For whoever does the will of my Father in heaven is my brother and sister and mother." Those who have given themselves to God are thus able to participate in the Father/Son relationship. The Church accepts the Yes that accompanies a gift of self, just as the Father accepted Mary's Yes, in order to admit those who say Yes into the heavenly fruitfulness of the eternal Yes between Father, Son, and Spirit.

God formed Eve from Adam's rib so that she

might be his essentially equal companion. But in the Old Testament, aside from a few episodes, women stay in the background, just as the Son and Spirit stay hidden behind the Father. Then, suddenly, Mary and the Church come to the fore at the same time. Through the Redeemer, the Virgin becomes Mother and the Church becomes bride and all the relations of creation are established anew because its feminine half shines forth in the arrival of the Son and in the Father's affirmation of everything: the fruitfulness of the Church depends on the Virgin, and she depends on the fruitfulness of heavenly grace. This, in turn, was necessary in order for the Father to acquire the face befitting him in the teachings of the Church as the first Person of the triune God.

In the Old Testament, a few great female figures come to the fore, but they are somehow always to one side and never in the great line of the prophets, of revelation. They leave their mark on a family, an episode, and even on an atrocious deed. After Mary, however, it is different. Even though women are not spoken of much in the Gospel, they nonetheless are absorbed into the Church: in the task of ecclesial fruitfulness; in holding the Church together (despite the fact of their not holding office); in contributing to the Church's image of sanctity as the Church; in keeping devotion to the Mother of the Lord alive.

The Son has formed the Church in order to show to his Father, through his relationship to the Church, a relief image of heavenly love in the world. It is not a relationship that stops with Christ and the Church, for the Son wanted to erect in the Church a monument to the Father's love, to the triune love; he wanted to commemorate in his Eucharist how much the Father loves the world but also how much he loves the Son in the Holy Spirit and that he permits the Son to make this kind of self-gift to men. The life-breath of the Church, with all her sacraments and institutions, is eternal and comes from heaven; the Church can do nothing more than to impart something of this heavenly air. Considered in this way, she seems to be the means for our anchorage in the eternal. The relations between natural man and his pre- and afterworld are transient and wobbly; the relations of God in his Trinity and to the world are unchanging; they belong to eternal life. Without the Church, believing man would be in danger of tearing down into his own transience something that belongs to the eternal: he might be so enthusiastic about Christ that the Father and Spirit would be as good as meaningless to him; or he might marvel at God's grace in just one saint and let himself be satisfied with that; or he might consider the inner-divine relations measured simply against his own mood or inclination. The Church exists in order to ward off this danger. She is the supernatural family who places the individual in the right relations, the regulating agent who establishes the proper intimacy and the proper distance. The Church does not forbid private devotions, but through her common Mass she puts everything individualistic in its proper place. It would only become dangerous if one gave oneself over to personal contemplation and devotion to such an extent that attending ecclesial celebrations came to seem superfluous and the public character of these celebrations irreligious and disruptive.

In the Church, the Son showed to the Father a kind of counterbalance to sin. He did not, of course, have to redeem the original creation but a world that has erred because of sin. In place of the sin that humanity otherwise shows to God, the Son shows him the Church. This is most clear with the institution of the sacrament of Reconciliation on Easter day, which gives the redemption its ecclesial form. The Father now sees grace in place of guilt, and in place of the punishment that hung over Adam he sees penitence, which has taken on the form of grace. The Father recognizes this as the work of the Son, indeed, the Father and Son together send forth the Spirit, who seals the work as a sign, not only of the Father's acceptance of the world, but also of his acceptance of the Church, which has a right to the Spirit, who is to affirm everything; to the Son, who has given the Church his body; and to the assenting Father, who gives himself to the redeemed world in standing by the Son and Spirit in the Church.

VIII

PRAYER AND THE FATHER'S SILENCE

When a human being comes to know the heavenly
Father, a conversation begins between them that is
known as prayer. What man says is a question to
God; what God says is an answer. The first words
penetrate something that existed from eternity, before words ever did. This something is like an eternal silence, though it was forever the exchange of
love between Father and Son in the Spirit, an exchange in which the Son may well be the eternal
Word of the Father and the Spirit signify the exchange of love but in which the word of love had
not been heard by man, who did not yet even exist.
When we penetrate this zone of eternity with our
questioning words of prayer, we can imagine how
God the Father kept silence with the Son (who is
the Word) and with the Spirit for an eternity, because God needs no words to love himself and to
realize his tri-personal will. The first spoken word
signified that, by taking hold of man, the intercourse
of eternity had acquired a new look. Henceforth, it
could be apprehended and transmitted as a spoken,
revealed word. The act of creation is thus connected
to the act of the creative, spoken word.

In the age of the Old Testament, God speaks to and through the prophets; he lets them accept and pass on the word; they are his mouthpieces; at the very most, they can translate the word into a form intelligible to man, but in no event can they touch or alter its meaning. In doing this, they are previews, or examples, and precursors of the Son. And the Mother of the Lord is included among them: when she conceives the Son who is the Word, brings him into the world, and rears him, she accepts the word as it was always intended and does not alter it through her acceptance. She may neither touch it in a way that would give it a different meaning nor impose her own meaning upon it. The word remains the word with its perfectly divine meaning, which it has had for all eternity. It was unto this conclusive acceptance by the Mother that the prophets received the word. It was not yet a bodily acceptance, but theirs was already a long-term relationship with the word. Far from being done with it once they spoke it, the prophets had then to attend to its fate; to see what was to become of it; to exhort the people to keep the word; perhaps even to remind themselves of exactly what it was and was not that they had said. And yet, once they had spoken and released the word, they did not have the opportunity to nurture it unfailingly to maturity as Mary would with the grace of the Father and with the help of the Holy Spirit.

But God relates to the world, not just in speech, but also in silence. This silence is in no sense a rupture in the relationship but rather the continuation of that which was the Father's togetherness with the Son in the Holy Spirit in eternity before the creation: one being in love. That does not change, as far as God is concerned, when Adam, after his sin, no longer hears God; nor does it change when Adam begins his long repentance. God's silent love has merely acquired a new form. Hitherto, it was met with reciprocal love; it was accustomed to being accepted completely and given back without measure. It is now met with the resistance of sin and has to struggle against this resistance in an express form of words. The word that the Father sends into the world after sin has the character of struggle and conquest, be it in the word of the prophets, in the word of the Son in the New Testament, or in the mission of the Spirit. A contradiction has always to be fought down for the purpose of a return and a drawing back into the Father's silence.

The silence of the Father is perfect fullness. When the Son talks of the one necessary thing—hearing his word—he may well give our prayer the form of words so that we can adapt ourselves to the infinity of God by using our own finite means. At the same time, however, he positions our prayer in the eternal silence, for the ultimate unfolding of the word is no longer audible. Our word continues to take effect in

silence; it becomes fruitful in silence. It is in silence
that the believer is accepted into the Father's being.
It is in the silence of the Christian that the most
profound encounter between Creator and creature
takes place.

The Father has never ceased to reveal himself; the
Incarnation of the Son was just one form of his manifestation, albeit an especially pressing form since
God became one among us. Even where the word
of God is not to be heard, God remains in the state
of revealing himself; his silence and his word have
the same force of mediation, just on different levels.
The nonbeliever has no clue about God's silence. He
is a doubter, so his call to God is like a challenge: if
he exists, he must make himself heard, work some
sign, which the believer thinks he needs in order to
be convinced of God's existence. For the believer,
the silence of God reveals his existence. He seeks to
find him in his silence; he presents himself to the
God who is in such a way that God does not need
to turn his being outward in order to be heard. It
is therefore a grace of participation in God's being
God when the believer feels himself invited to contemplate God in silence. The believer is silent, but
God too is silent; and the believer is not silent out
of a need to make himself noticeable through his
silence but rather with the intention of being conformed to God and of not being considered in any
way by God other than in that which he desires. If
he really succeeds in praying silently and in silenc-

ing his wishes, thoughts, imagination, and very self, he will be so emptied and calm that he will find the entrance to God's eternal nature, which God reveals to him in silence. A person at prayer is neither lethargic nor impassive but rather extremely alert to accepting what God shows him, that is, ultimately, his divine being in his silence, his being thus and not otherwise. The believer observes God in his divine nature, and this observation is love; for what the person at prayer is pursuing is nothing other than the exchange of triune love, which in itself is so full that it is not disturbed when the world at prayer comes to participate in it.

When a man of prayer decides to leave everything in order to enter the solitariness of pure prayer, the *contemplative life*, he is aware of only being able to do so because of the immediate strength of God's silence. He has heard the word of God that has called him; he has also probably given an audible Yes in reply. Once his choice of life has been purified before God and the life of contemplation begins, he stands before God's silence and is at its disposal. His striving and contemplation lead to this silence. Like the first monks who went into the desert, he will today deny himself all the things that he has built up around him—a life governed by his surroundings, friends, habits, and family—in order to experience from God himself his new destiny in emptiness. He frees himself from everything in which his life was enmeshed in order to offer his simple self to God in the hope that this self will vanish before and into God's greatness. He no longer wants to be taken into account, nor does he want special treatment from God; he would like simply, in a paltry imitation of the Son's self-submitting will, to adjust himself so completely to the will of the Father that this silent will alone will henceforth reign over him.

He will no longer be concerned with the accomplishments of particular days or measures of time but rather, as he prays silently, will come to participate in the silence of God, which expresses itself in no other way than in eternity. He does not know his final hour, but this should not be a boundary stone for him because he harbors the hope of accompanying God's eternity in each and every hour in unswerving fidelity, of being a vessel for God's eternity to such an extent that his final hour need not be noticed especially or his prayer interrupted, almost as if he wanted to prevent God interrupting for his sake what he would otherwise be doing at that moment. He thus hopes that his life will pass into eternity as good as unnoticed, the eternity in which it has already had a share through silent prayer.

The external obligations of monastic life, the community with its offices, and a certain link to the outside world need not be felt as disturbances. God has created the man of prayer to be a man among men, and the Son's commandment of love extends to all. But these external things are accomplished from and in prayer in such a way that they can aid the contemplation of God's silence. The life that is sacrificed for the brothers and the self-denial of a good many things out of love for them belong to silent prayer. An obligation cannot be imposed on someone else because a certain brother wants to pray and be left in peace all the time. What he does for the others, he likewise does for God in order to forge a path for them to God. If he succeeds in living in this unity of silent prayer, he is a true imitator of the Son. And were he a priest and had to act as confessor in the monastery, he would know that his actions were a participation in the active life of the Son, though within the life of contemplation. For the division of his time need not be the same externally as that in the life of Jesus, and Jesus, too, must have performed many works of love for his fellowmen during the hidden years of his life. In the life of the Lord, the decisive point between contemplation and action is uniquely visible. In the life of the monk, there can be innumerable little such points, perhaps above all because he is not holy enough to endure one big decisive point, because he needs the mixture, the variation, indeed, the monastic form of life approved by the Church in order to make his silent way to God amid the communion of saints, while in his solitariness nonetheless preserving his share in the office and Church as befits the Christian.

In each and every prayer, even the most fleeting of pleas to God for help, it is faith that takes the lead. This means that man has to leave the answer to his prayers up to God and, also, that even if God answers the prayer in the way he hoped and perhaps sends the desired help or solution, he will nonetheless never survey the invisible path that his prayer takes on its way to being granted, nor will he ever be able to explain it to anyone else. It is therefore not astonishing for believers when God answers their prayers in a way other than that for which they hoped. It may be that the difficulty that they would have liked to have had solved must remain unsolved. And thus believers may place their petitions quite simply before the silence of God and, in faith, have to take this silence as their answer. Faith, which knows that it stands before the silence of God, is content with this. Faith knows that God cannot have done anything other than hear the prayer and that he has accepted the words of the person at prayer into his silence. If the praying believer truly knows this, he has already advanced from where he was when he began praying: he no longer thinks that God has to help him out with his narrow concern; he is convinced that everything is all right as it is. Whenever God gives man an insight into the significance of his silence, his faith is widened and God's participation in his faith deepened. If a person prays for the Church, that is, for a concern to which he knows himself to be connected through the communion of saints, the granting of his prayer will probably go unheeded on a personal level. In this he experiences that the concerns of the Church—her thriving, the help that God gives to her—are far more manifold than he can imagine. The Church reaches across the whole world; her concerns—even though they can be reduced to formulae—are so expansive that they cannot be judged from a single viewpoint. Anyone who prays as the Church prays takes into account from the outset that he will not be able to oversee how his prayer is granted, regardless of his love and commitment. The prayer concern, the prayer itself, and the granting of the prayer are played out in a sphere that is removed from human scrutiny. And yet, the faith of the man of prayer does seek to become efficacious in this sphere; indeed, in such a way that he is aware of the infinite efficacy of God's silence and serves this silence with his own helpless silence. He lets God act alone and entrusts his prayer to him; he places it gratuitously into the grace of God. In this way he is taken one step farther within God's silence.

But it might also be the case that a man of prayer comes to regard his daily prayer time, as well as the number of his fleeting prayers, as insufficient in comparison with the time that he has at his disposal, that is, the duration of his entire human life. There is, of course, also the option to dispose of himself—

the man created by God—as he chooses. He therefore devises the plan of giving everything to God.
He places himself with everything he has before the
silence of God, which is nowhere more abundantly
obvious than in contemplation. A person who does
this takes his life out of the control that the believer always dispenses of for the duration and effect of an individual prayer. The purpose of his life
is now to belong to God completely, and the means
to achieve this end is the life of the counsels, in
which one obediently denies one's own will. Upon
entering the community of a religious order, this
person still has some idea of who he is and what he
is giving up: his time, his possessions, his very self.
But he does not know what God, in the silence in
which he too will be able to participate, will make
of him and what is his. He who he is now is not
who he will continue to be. Time and possessions
will be transformed. Something that can be called
sacrifice is the basis at the origin of the contemplative life, but sacrifice is not the same as the contemplative life. The individual's Yes is a promise, but
it is not the same as keeping the promise. And the
God to whom the person entering the religious life
makes his gift of self is not necessarily the same as
the one he will come to know during his contemplative life. Contemplation, as God's invitation to
participate in his silence, is something infinitely bigger and more inscrutable than could ever be guessed

or judged from the outside. The individual takes the risk of hoping to be accepted by God in such a way that God himself, through his grace, will let that which is best pleasing to him come into existence out of the so-called sacrifice. But in expressing his basic consent, the individual's sacrifice has probably already lost most of its character, because for him the sacrifice means the denial of something he knows, whereas the contemplative life is already removed from everything he knows: for God is ever forming the life of the man of prayer out of the fullness of his silence; he constantly makes unknown things out of it by putting it to use, but the individual knows neither the place where his prayer is put to use nor his own place in it. He has entrusted to God what he used to have at his own disposal; God now lets man have at his disposal the concerns of his Church and of the world to be redeemed, but without ever linking him unambiguously to a particular realm that he might perhaps otherwise have entrusted to him. What God demands is prayer and nothing else: pure self-gift. But this mere prayer, this naked gift of self, signifies the most extreme laying bare; it is humanity existing without anything extra, humanity standing before God with all possible supplications of prayer, all of which he accepts in a silence in which they become completely unimportant. If the person praying was hitherto bound to a specific task, this bond is now loosed, but in an inscrutable way. This is necessary if the person is not to find God in the disparate tasks assigned to him by God but rather to grow ever more in his recognition of the triune God until nothing more stands between him and God and the relationship has become so close that the points of connection have grown invisible. God thanks the individual for his gift of self by concealing him in his perfect silence; indeed, his silence intensifies to such a point that the individual can no longer hear God. This ultimate intensification is the "dark night", where the individual becomes so fulfilled in contemplation of God that the Father transports him to the site of the crucifixion, where the Son cries out to the Father for having forsaken him.

Looking back from here it can once again be seen that with even the simplest prayer, one embarks into what is inscrutable and unanswerable. Whenever we have some human difficulty, we can appeal to our fellowmen with a question or for help in the hope that what is hard for us will seem remediable to someone else. If one turns with the same difficulty to God, with a hope that must already be a Christian hope, one is already moving in a sphere that surpasses mere human fulfillment and leaves free the manner in which the problem is to be solved. This sphere is accessible to faith alone.

～

Man was created by God with the ability to hear him. He can talk with God as with a fellow human being by means of question and answer. He feels the adequacy of the answer; he hears the word of the Father; and he knows that he is being guided by God. This guidance is a gracious participation in the contemplative attitude of God, who on the seventh day ceased to work actively as Creator and henceforth walks in Paradise, so to speak, contemplating his work. Activity is now left up to man, who has to head for where God is walking. However, instead of allowing himself to be guided there, man sinks into the false activity of sinning and thus hiding himself from God. As a result, the relationship is reversed once more: God becomes active so that man can become contemplative and let things be done.

Sin has caused man's inability to guide himself. The Son sets his perfect obedience to the Father against sin and thereby restores to men their ability to be guided by God. This is realized above all in contemplation, where, in total devotion, man frees himself for God's guidance and no longer brings into play either his reason or his wish to hear adequate answers to each of his questions.

The Son, of whom it is written that no one has seen God except him, possesses, as man, the vision of the Father. This does not prevent him from being perfectly obedient to the Father. In his vision, he seeks nothing other than the will of the Father.

He does not feel himself in any way relieved of the obligation to obedience on the grounds of his vision. Instead, it drives him to be even more obedient wherever possible. As God, he does not need this encouragement, but, as man, he gives it to us, not by communicating his vision, but rather by bestowing the gift of contemplation, which is the means of hearing the paternal will more clearly and executing it, not in a way that is of benefit to us, but rather in a ceaseless gift of self to the Church, the bride of the Lord.

God is free to visit visions upon a contemplative. He can transform faith's nonvision into a vision bestowed by him. But this, too, belongs to his silence insofar as he also hides himself behind the vision that he gives, that is, he sends his revelation, not as a situation with which the believer can come to terms as he would with a complete fact, but rather supplied with the character of a mystery. The believer is shown things that have significance for the Church and for the collective well-being of the faith in the world; as an exception he might also be shown something that is of importance to himself, be it a vision or a voice that comforts him or transports him from one condition into another as desired by God. But this something that is intended for him personally presupposes that he has a special mission, indeed, that his personal vision has meaning for the faith of the whole—a meaning that in the moment of its revelation may well not be unveiled but that nonetheless is related to the mission of the person to whom it has been given. God makes a gift to him in order to make a gift to others; God goes through and beyond him in order to reveal something for which God needs him as an instrument. But God never shows himself without mediation, because the vision must be apprehended out of silence. In its ultimate origin, this silence is the silence of the Father at the Cross; it is the fact that he does not answer the Son's question, the Son who no longer sees him although he is certain of the Resurrection right into the midst of his suffering. For when he promises Paradise to the thief, he also promises something that he knows and that assumes its place within his knowledge of the things of God, even when he himself is robbed of it in that moment through his suffering and obedience. Between the promise to the thief and the cry to the Father there is a period of time during which all the Son's felt certainty is withdrawn. But the Father sends his silence in and into this withdrawal, that is, the certainties of his heavenly life in which he reveals himself as the one who is veiled; he steps forth as the one who is hidden; and he is present as the one who is silent; as if he were withdrawing into his justice solely in order to make tangible the love of the Son who has redeemed the world.

It is because this love of the Son was borne bodily by the human being Mary that the Mother of God plays such a great role in the visions of the contemplative. The inner life of the Church is formed immediately from her life. The contemplative receives a share in the contemplation of the Mother as she awaits her Son, in the encounters between Mother and Son, and in the Church's coming into being in the many situations of Mary's life. The Father remains silently in the background just as he is silent when the Spirit descends upon Mary. He is silent because his will will now be fulfilled by the Spirit, by the Son, and by a faithful humanity.

~

A person deciding to enter the contemplative life knows—albeit without being able to formulate it exactly or to guess how it is going to work out— that God is leading him to a true life that will alter him without fail. However, this transformation that God will carry out in him is also offered in another form to those who are to lead a Christian life in the world. All the faithful experience a new birth through Christ in Baptism, and in this world they can already receive and experience a share of what God is keeping in reserve for those who are his. The contemplative becomes an entirely new person when he makes his gift of self. Likewise, the Christian living in the world (who perhaps places value on remaining the same person he knows himself to be) nonetheless does not want to relinquish the possibility of being transformed by God. In his own state of life, he will be on the lookout for the means to become—for his own sake but more for the sake of the world around him—the person whom God wants him to be. He knows that he will be incapable of communicating anything divine that he has not already received in the proper way and that, in order to be able to receive it, he must conform to God's gift.

The share that he takes, and the transformation that takes place in him, are things that can be experienced, that belong closely together, but that nonetheless do not form a scrutable whole because they are a part of the work that God enacts from his eternity to eternity. A believer can improve himself, diminish his faults, pray more joyfully, and set time aside for daily contemplation. But he cannot measure the progress that he makes any more than he can observe the manner in which God acts within him. He merely knows that he is participating in the mystery of God's silence. Through his prayer and effort, but far more through the Son's grace surrounding him, he is elevated into a region of the Father that belongs to the Father so completely that he even gains a share in the Father's hiddenness. He becomes so completely alienated from himself that, were he to go in search of himself, he would probably find something, but it would no longer be the self he knew. At the very most it would be something that was an obstacle to God for, as something established and familiar, it would be holding itself back from the workings of God. He therefore has to give his assent to the unknown ways in which God works, and the consequences of this assent will without fail extend much farther than he thinks, for his Yes proceeds fundamentally into the sphere of the hidden God.

In his apostolate, he will try to make Christianity more attractive. But there is a greater sphere to his apostolic work whose manner of working escapes him. Transient life cannot desire to exercise control over eternal life. The former knows about the latter, looks forward to it, and, in the best case, already has a share in it in the here and now, in a measure determined by eternal life. Man, who is neither able nor should desire ever to control God in any way should find his joy in already being together with God on earth in a form that is unfathomable to him; indeed, man should find joy in the fact that he is the property of eternity.

God's "ever more" takes effect throughout the entire realm of contemplative prayer. This is also to be known in the active life, and man must seek to insert himself into it, not in such a way that he no longer knows his own striving and affirmation, but rather in a "letting it be done" that has a well-supported earthly foundation in created reality, in faith, and in the Church—all of which, however, are to open out onto the unfathomableness of God. This relationship can be read in every single word that Christ spoke. We are able to understand these words; they are commandments, admonitions, or instructions, but ultimately they always cross over into a region of silence for their fulfillment. The entire figure of Christ, which we can contemplate and accompany on earth, remains shrouded in the Father's silence, which is transparent only to the Son. And at the end of his course, the Son who has become visible—the Word become audible—also returns to silence. Out of the general silence of the Father, Son, and Spirit, we are to experience greater things than ever before about the triune God. In his earthly form, the Word of God shared in the fact that there are boundaries to human words. As soon as he once again speaks alone before the Father, in order to be audible for us through him, he once again has the absolute form of the Father's infinity. The Word is spoken into the Father's silence and is absorbed by it in such a way that man is only able to hear him when silent, that is, when conformed by grace to the world of eternal life.

When one views, in faith, a person who has just died, a person who until a little while ago was still moving and speaking yet who now lies motionless and silent, this change alienates us far more than when we view some lifeless thing. But we pray beside the coffin, and this prayer participates in the deceased's first silence before God. It accompanies him to God and is a way by which the Church proves her vitality to the Son by accompanying the deceased beyond the realm of time to God. The Church herself is not silence; but she carries the silent deceased in the heart of her prayer. She will not make any attempt to snatch just one more word from the deceased or to attack the words he spoke on earth in order to hold them against him into eternity. Instead, she reaches for her liturgical prayer, the word that is valid for each and all in this situation, so that God will acknowledge the validity of the Church's escort and accept the deceased as a brother of Christ. The prayers for the dead are an expression of the Church's knowledge of God's silence, which is draped over the deceased like a shroud. The deceased may have been accustomed to contemplative prayer and to a kind of rehearsal for the vision of the silent God. Death now carries him into the open vision of eternity; and, in the passage through judgment and its purification, the ability to behold this vision is bestowed upon him.

IX

PRAYER AND THE WORD
OF THE FATHER

Everything has divine significance where God dwells with God. The word and the silence and everything that unites God with God have an import that is divine and understandable to God alone. Adam's experience of God, however, is the origin of experience. Adam is the one who has just emerged from God's hand, and his first memory concerns his being with God in a totally new and good world. It is good because God has deemed it thus: out of the Father's work, Son and Spirit have experienced the good and have agreed with him. The first man stands pure in the world, but the inner-divine intercourse has not yet been opened up to him. He is in a rank of his own and is content, without worry and without curiosity. In the goodness of his being as man, he stands simply before the eternal being of the Father.

However, once sin has altered, not just man, but also the whole of creation, he has to start seeking what he has rejected, namely, the good; and, together with this good, he must seek God. Man himself has forfeited his language because he has utilized it for sin, and, as a result, all his words are imprisoned by a strange finitude and boundedness. They suffice to express what he means. But they are altered words; his state of sin, his mortality, and his exclusion from Paradise mark the character of his words. He speaks a language that knows the wrath of God, that knows what it means to turn away, and that knows death. It is a language that is not only in the mouth of a sinner but that has become inwardly suited to depicting his fault, indeed, to its furthering and multiplication. And, having reconstructed the words he speaks, he does the same for his hearing; he gets used to at best guessing from the words of others what he himself might have been able or have wanted to express.

God's language does not change. For his is the same from eternity. However, when God goes over to using human words, man can at first grasp them only in relation to his own sinfulness. He now possesses only a thoroughly weak ability to give credit to the word of God as it is spoken to him and to allow it a more than human significance; to let it, not just unfold and bear fruit in a merely human sense, but also to concede from the outset that, as the bearer of the total divine truth, it means infinitely more than man can know. When he speaks with God—in prayer—he puts his altered human words before the absolutely true divine Word, the inadequate before the adequate, the insufficient and bounded before the perfect and unbounded, indeed, his own misunderstanding before the fullness of wisdom and knowledge of the Holy Spirit and of the entire triune God.

Misunderstandings are bound to occur again and again when human words encounter the word of God prior to the manifestation of the Son. The two do not yet totally fit together. What man hears is not entirely what God wants to say. It is because of this that the Son, as Word of the Father, becomes man. He remains the infinite Word of the Father with the full substance of truth that eternity gives to the Word, and, nonetheless, he becomes a man among us, a man with our habits and subject to our laws. He learns to make himself intelligible as man, as everyone has to do when he is growing up. He hears words that have earthly meaning from his Mother and from his neighbors, from his apostles as well as from his persecutors. And, as the Word of the Father, he himself speaks the earthly language: others hear and understand him. But his words have a resonance that extends beyond everything they know. Likewise, he hears and understands the words of others, but he absorbs them in a way that makes them become words that are suited to God. He thus allows himself to become a changer, a transformer of words: by becoming man as God, he becomes, as "Word of the Father", the "Word of Man". An entirely new situation results from this for prayer, because man can now express in faith his finite and bounded words so that, through the Son, they gain validity before the countenance of the Father. But these words cannot themselves be changed in the Son without a concomitant change taking place in the person who uttered them. The hope that accompanies human words into the Son is the same hope through which human beings transform themselves more profoundly into Christians. More than ever before, their words of prayer become active, fruitful words.

∼

As the trustee and transformer of the words exchanged between God and man, the Son gives his bride, the Church, a similar and complementary function. Indeed, he shapes her in his own image. He places things within her that originate from his mystery with the Father and with the Spirit but that are to be communicated to man, and the Church is made capable of this communication. At her heart is the sacrament of transformation through the word that is given and accepted by God, through which bread and wine become Christ's Body and Blood. All who receive this Body are confirmed as being his members. The Body of the Word of God is something concrete that becomes *super-concrete* through the words of consecration. The Word breaks his boundaries so that he becomes, for all, the Body that confers a share in the eternity of the infinite God.

However, the believer understands in faith that, hidden in the species of bread and wine, an act of God is taking place that is absolute and that transforms everything, an act that is meant for him, the earthly man, who as a whole is to become a member of Christ in the Church.

Man does not live from bread alone, nor does the believer live from the Eucharist alone. His prayer, as words, undergoes transformation in the Son, but this transformation has an ecclesial side as well. The believer commends his words to the Son and to the Church for acceptance, and the exchange between them both is a mystery of love. Neither is harmed by the reception of the other. It corresponds to the will of the Son that the Church, which he created for himself, should receive it too. Out of the prayers that the Church has accepted, he forms a treasure, a treasury of prayer, that is, not just distributed as it pleases the triune God, but rather simultaneously bears witness to the fact that the faithful stand together in solidarity for one another. Each and every believer is supported by the treasury of prayer so that, in the Church, those who pray and those who do not pray gain a certain share in the transformation in the Son by being his members in the Church. The word of prayer is fruitful in one's fellowman, and this fruitfulness is the expression of the Son's commandment of love become fact.

The Son becomes manifest in the world as the expression of the Father's fruitfulness, which will bestow his word with force and resonance. The Son will make a gift of himself, and, in taking men back to the Father, he takes himself back by letting his fruitful word act within them. The Word thus becomes their door to the Father. The Word has divulged himself in the redemption as much as was pleasing to the Father; the ultimate revelation of his fruitfulness will take place, however, in heaven.

Something corresponding to this happens in the Church as the communion of saints that has been ordained by the Word. All who believe are bound to others through the Word. At the same time, this bond is a divulgence, albeit not a complete one, but one carried out to the extent that it is necessary *for*, and required by, the Word. It is from one another that the faithful know faith to have the same life significance for them all, keeping them in the Church and prompting their ecclesial actions and their reception of the sacraments. But the divulgence goes no farther; the ultimate mysteries of the Word are played out in man in a sphere that is closed to others. For the true believer, this withdrawn sphere corresponds to the sphere that will undergo its mighty expansion in heaven.

Although the Church, in her comprehensive unity as the communion of saints, signifies the Son's continuing life on earth, this signification is also accomplished, on the other hand, by individual Christians who each reflect something of the uniqueness of the only begotten Son of the Father. For the Son too, like all men, lived an individual and unrepeatable human life. And the universally valid word that the Son molds for, and gives to, the Church is not abstract because, as such, it would be finite. Rather it is a fully concrete and hence ever unique word that thus strikes every unique man in his concreteness. In God, it is apprehended perfectly but infinitely; only an inkling of its infinity lives in man. However, it is not true that the individual words that the Son gives to the Church or to the individual believer break the form of temporality on the grounds of their eternal content, as if they had to be stretched out until they were the size of eternity and their meaning extended far enough beyond human words that they became infinite. Rather, the word of Christ that has been placed into time has full validity in the face of the triune God, and, because of this validity, it is capable of eternity without ever losing its temporal uniqueness. Indeed, it may very well correspond to eternity, not through a dilation, but through a concentration of its meaning.

Mary's Yes helps to clarify this mystery. Seen from her perspective, her Yes is a single and unique word uttered in her unique situation from which it cannot be detached. Nonetheless, it corresponds in the face of God, whose very concreteness and absoluteness appears through this one word. Indeed, Mary experiences this concreteness as God's similarly unique response: the only begotten Word of the Father will be born of her. And she remains the only one who will be the bodily mother of the Lord. She bears the child as an answer to her prayer and as a spur to ours. It is her task to point out just how concrete God's answers are.

When the Son institutes the Church, he elevates Mary into the state of spiritual bridehood while he himself becomes the Bridegroom. There is, therefore, a further development in his relationship to his Mother—that is, the Church—and there is an invitation to all to follow in Mary's footsteps in prayer. Henceforth, the praying Christian will effect an arrival of the Lord through his prayer, and this will take effect in the Church in a way that is parallel to the birth from the Mother. Her *fiat* becomes a *fiat* of the whole Church, not within an anonymous mass, but within a community of persons who retain their distinctiveness before God. Ecclesial office may well be strengthened through prayer, but the individual's attitude toward, and his works before, God are strengthened no less and perhaps more than the office—albeit supported by the Church, since all prayers are ecclesial but with the individual as the goal. Thus, what the singling out of individual saints within the communion of saints is all about is the gravity of an individual mission within the Church's common task. When God becomes man, he appears in the utmost personalness; for no one is more personal than God.

In the New Testament, the Son is the Word, the voice of the Father. When this Word is compared with the word of God in the Old Testament, the Son emerges as an intensification because he comes into the world laden with the whole of heavenly love. In the Old Testament, the Father put into words his relationship to the world; in the New Testament, the Son brings triune divine love. But there is, in the word of the Father mediated by the Son, not only the spoken word, but also the discreet word, the word of intimacy, which exists but remains unspoken, which perhaps makes itself known in joy or reveals itself in an attitude but which is never audibly expressed. When the Father speaks, he is simultaneously silent. This simultaneity expresses the being of the Son who remains the Word both in speech and in silence. Ultimately, it expresses God's "ever greater being" in relation to man. God is not only omnipresent; he can also do something *contrary* within the unity that befits his nature. When a mother commands her child to go somewhere, the child gets going on his way, not merely so long as he can hear his mother's words, but right until he reaches his destination. The child is bound in obedience to his mother's words. This applies to a far higher degree to the Son, who adheres to the Father's word of mission, which he alone can hear, right to his destination—death on the Cross. This means everything together: the suffering, the fear, the silence of heaven. When a Christian prays, he likewise hears God above and beyond his express word. Much is done that is unsaid to him and to the Church and that yet requires and accompanies him on his way. His faith grows in the unheard word of God; his love is strengthened and his hope ignited by it. These are deeds of the silent God, deeds that stand there as concrete, graspable consequences of Lord's proclamation, "Knock, and it will be opened to you." Man is not being told continually to believe more, to love more, or to hope more; God lets him believe, love, and hope more because he prays. God increases the virtue that yearns for him by accepting the words of prayer into his divine silence and returning them as deeds; deeds for which the individual cannot account but deeds of which the Church takes note because the effects of one pass to all; the increased faith of one bears fruit in all; and the communion of saints is built up in and through the word of the Father. And the Son is revealed each and every time.

X

THE INVITATION OF
THE TRIUNE GOD

God in heaven decides on the Incarnation of the Son
because man has fallen into sin. The Father has created the world; the Son puts himself at the Father's
disposal in order to redeem the world. But the Son
is not the only one who is active in this offer; the
Father is equally active by inviting the Son to the
redemption and knowing of his coming Incarnation.
An invitation of this kind from the Father is also issued by the Son to all who will become brothers of
the Lord through the Incarnation and will be able to
cooperate in his work in their own way. The Son's
decision will, at the right time, *co-demand* individual
people; in eternity, however, this decision is made
in the harmony of the three Persons and in its full
consequence for humanity. If we, being redeemed
by him and to a degree living with him, are able
to have some inkling of the Son's role in this, it
is not without some knowledge of the role of the
Holy Spirit. He will emerge at the overshadowing
of the Mother and is sent forth after the Son's return to the Father: his task in the triune decision is
made somewhat visible to us in his role as bearer and

mediator at the beginning and in his role of obedience at the end. And, as the expression of the love between Father and Son, he is also forever the one who enacts the decision of salvation and the witness to the entire event whose testimony is simultaneously its realization. Father and Son can look to him in order to read from him what the reality of this work should be; in eternity, he is the bearer of the triune purpose. And thus the Father, too, can already contemplate the Son as invited man just as he contemplates the Son's arrival in the flesh from the perspective of eternity and of its presence.

Throughout the whole of the Old Testament, God constantly issues an invitation to men to turn to him. The words of the prophets contain an amalgamation of this invitation. Both man, who hears the voice of the prophet, and the prophet, who hears the voice of God, know the ineluctable seriousness of this demand from God. Even the words of prophecy that relate to future things are a warning and an invitation, as corresponds to the conditions in which men find themselves after the fall.

The arrival of the Son transforms the meaning of the invitation. The Son now invites others as the one who has himself been invited, the one who from eternity knows, accepts, and realizes the Father's invitation. And the tidings that he directs at men are nothing more than this same invitation that has been issued to him, into which he now invites men as well—though admittedly at some distance. For to the Son, as man, his work signifies a precise demand, which he recognizes and which is, as such, the most absolute excessive demand possible. He will carry out the work of this excessive demand in restless obedience, and it will constantly be "ever more" than the Father can expect. In contrast, men are invited as sinners. They cannot in any way gauge the "ever more" into which they are placed. It quite simply surpasses them, and, having been surpassed, they are drawn into the "ever more" of the Son. He will bear and make up the difference in what even his best disciples, the greatest saints, could not do.

An invitation from the Father can be contemplated in every word spoken by the Son, in every parable, and in every prayer. And the whole space consecrated to the silence of the Father, and to the mystery in which he hides as he reveals himself, is present in them as well. The Father reveals the truth of his being, the urgency of his demand, and the paths to its fulfillment (paths that all lead through the Son), but he keeps himself hidden behind the Son in order that the Son's arrival might retain its complete fullness among men as well. The individual can neither see nor realize this fullness, but the Church is entrusted with bringing it into sight and to realization, both of which the Son bequeaths to her as his legacy: his vision and his fulfillment. She can dispose of them as with a possession that has been bequeathed to her as her own (even though she can transmit Christ's vision in nothing but definitions of faith); and it is a possession for which no one can account. The Church, as institution, can say that she has received sight from the Lord, but, in the same breath, she has to admit, perhaps with great reluctance, to her inability to see. She sees to the extent that a bride may see what the bridegroom sees; she does not see to the extent that, as institution, she is not a person and does not have human eyes with which to see what is shown openly to her or to mediate it in this form.

In making Mary the prototype for his bride, the Church, it must mean that the Son wants, first, to bestow what the Mother means to him with a general value and duration and, secondly, to perpetuate for the duration of the world her maternal task with regard to him but now in relation to man. However, it is now that Mary's life of nonvision begins: she keeps herself pure, ready, and free for God and the task he gives her; and when this is made known to her in the encounter with the angel— surprisingly and unexpectedly—she gives herself to it completely. The vision of the angel is a binding vision for her; it is the spoken word of God, which (as always) is as intelligible to man as is required but which otherwise remains, as vision and as word, entwined in an infinite seam of mystery that rests in

God. After the overshadowing, the vision is withdrawn from the Mother; she has the Son within her as her mystery, the Son who does possess the vision; she knows that she is bearing him even when, for a while, she does not yet feel him; then she gets used to carrying him and conforms to his movements and needs in order to give birth to him in the manner God desires of her. The fact that she does not see constitutes a steadfast knowledge; she knows about God's dwelling within her, and she also knows that her life belongs to this mystery and that her Son, whom she is now shaping in body, is shaping her in spirit. Her occupation with him in nonvision will enable her to see him according to the will of God: with physical eyes but, at the same time, in a spiritual vision of his nature. Her eyes will be a likeness of her readiness, of her inner self-gift, and of her letting the will and teaching of the Son be done. In her, the vision (and all Christian vision is meant in this way!) will constantly increase her faith, extending it to things with which it seems to have nothing to do; there are no strict distinctions between everyday and holiday, between domestic and ecclesial tasks, between the world of knowledge and the world of faith. Everything that projects into the life of the Mother acquires a relationship to her living faith and goes through her faith into the vision of the Father that the Son possesses. As the bride of Christ, she sees what the Bridegroom desires of her, but the eternal extent of his demands, and their unfolding in the triune God, is seen by the Son alone.

When the bride now expressly becomes the Church, she takes on these characteristics of Mary. When Peter, in order to be able to assume his office, answers the threefold question concerning his greater love and thereby receives the love of John[1] within himself and steps into his place, he equally takes within himself the relationship of love between John and Mary that the Lord decreed on the Cross. He absorbs within himself her immediate vision of the Crucified, which has, however, been taken away from him; he absorbs it within himself in order to affirm, to stamp, and to define it in terms and phrases that have complete universal validity and are code-termined through his absorption of John, not only of the John at the foot of the Cross, but of the John of the future, mysterious Revelation.[2] He absorbs the visionary John in both forms, and this vision belongs to him: John is his eye, and Peter is made able within himself to see while yet not seeing. In contrast, John, as he sees, will not see, because the

[1] Cf. Adrienne von Speyr, *Johannes*, vol. 4 (Einsiedeln: Johannes Verlag, 1949); English trans.: *The Birth of the Church: Meditations on John 18–21*, trans. by David Kipp (San Francisco, Ignatius Press, 1991). —ED.

[2] Cf. Adrienne von Speyr, *Apokalypse*, vol. 1 (Einsiedeln: Johannes Verlag, 1950).—ED.

official Church has taken from him the right to have the vision at his own disposal. He hands over what he has seen to the Church, and the Church administers this possession, which has become her own.

~

The Son fully accepted the invitation that was issued to him. Precisely as the God-Man, he knew how much was demanded of him and which answer was expected. From eternity, he knew himself to be the Word, and he also knew that, as the Word, he had to give the answer. As the Word, he wanted to give the answer to men out of love, not only to the work of the Father, but also to the Father himself: however manifold the ways in which the love of God pours forth into the world, it nonetheless always leads back to the love of God for God. In order to be able to invite men and to answer together with them in love, the Son first had to speak as man. He had to prove to the Father that man is truly capable of answering, and he also had to prove the same thing to men. He more and more divested himself of everything that was his own in order to die on the Cross, to die while still answering. Everyone was able to recognize that only the path of relinquishment can lead to the ultimate answer and that, even at the point at which strength is taken from man, the answer can still be given undiminished.

The Son has given his answer to God and to men: as an individual immediately to God, and as a member of humanity in union with all together. He has done this in order that each and every human being may feel doubly struck by the image of the crossed beams at the center of which he, the Man, himself has to take his place. And in order that this center not remain empty, the incarnate God has placed himself there. However, in order that the form of the Cross might have strength and validity for all, he has instituted the Church. The Church, as his bride, must receive and carry out his commandment of love without interruption and must bind man to man in such a way that both relationships are realized. For the Church is not only a unity as an institution and structure; she is also a unity in each individual who, as such, is invited and issued the same demand of love as is the Church as a whole. It is far from sufficient that all are invited and appear bound to the Yes of the Mother through the unity of the Church, which is the bride. In their immediacy before God, all must hear and answer vertically as well, regardless of what their neighbor does. One cannot merely latch onto the Church's answer; as the individual that one is, one must answer into the Church and cannot run from the Church with one's mission. This is the only way that the Cross can remain intact at the place where it must stand: in the Church.

The Church possesses through this Cross, not just universality (a "characteristic" that the individual can understand to some degree), but also a monumentality that exceeds all contemplation on the grounds of the nearly infinite number of all individuals whom she reflects and represents. This being the case, she becomes a true likeness of God's infinity precisely in this regard. She quite simply towers above the individual and becomes for him a concrete reference to God. God is not only ever greater than man (how could he be otherwise!), he is also greater than this mighty thing that I can scarcely contemplate in human terms—the bride of Christ. The Church, however, is not permitted to despair of herself because of God's infinity above her, since her Bridegroom is forever helping her above and beyond herself. She is charged with being the bride, and it would be unworthy of her to revoke her Yes, even for a moment, or to contemplate her boundaries and shield herself behind them. She should not say, "I would like to, but these Christians won't join in; I have so many apostates to deal with, and the rest are all just half-hearted; I am retiring to the purely religious and am leaving the worldly realm to others; my failure is so visible that I don't want to risk entering into dialogue here anymore; I still want to be the bride, but in my current state, I am not . . .".

Instead, the Church should know that she is the best thing that Christ has instituted and that she has to give her answer as he desires it of her—like the bride who gives herself to the bridegroom; like the artist's idea to be and to become what he wants. She is a projection of the Son's will, but only insofar as she remains the living bride. She is not supposed to represent something that was once upon a time; she has to be in order to become. She must not be like an empty cathedral that bears witness to a once glorious age; she must remain inhabited and in use; she must serve, not a God whom she bit by bit reduces to her own size, but the God who has brought her into being in order to lead her as is his unfathomable pleasure.

A person who has been challenged and receives a mission, who sees a path before him that he should take and who is getting himself ready to follow the Son, will see quite clearly that his answer will always remain weak and insufficient. And yet he knows that not only God will hear this answer and gather it into his grace but that it belongs to the task of the Church to give to his answer the necessary richness of tone. The Church, as the bride of Christ, has to complete what the individual begins within her. Every mission is a starting point, but every mission that is undertaken in earnest is perfected in the Church's superabundance, which she has been given as a bridal gift from the Son. The Church proceeds in the name and in the service of the Lord, even though she can never fully comprehend as a whole what it is that she has to do. She comprehends what she can formulate and determine. Ultimately, however, she does not comprehend (and this is a grace that the Lord has given her) how God can regard as complete what she has offered to him in bits and pieces.

The Church's lack of comprehension is not to be equated with an individual's lack of comprehension. The Christian who knows he has been called to take discipleship seriously also knows what he has to offer: he has his life, his future, his freedom, and his possessions. Yet he counts on grace, particularly on the blessing of religious vows, to keep to his promise as best as he can. He is aware that he will always lag behind the demands that are made of him, not just because of ascertainable faults, but also because of the many incalculable things that represent the distance between him and the Lord, the gulf between his promise and his ability to keep it. He has a clear awareness of having failed once and for all in an irreparable way. And he does not comprehend how God can nonetheless turn everything to the good and, moreover, needs him as an instrument even though he knows himself to be far too sluggish and unsuitable. The Church lags behind her task in a different way. Her lagging behind is constantly drowned out by perfection: God again and again makes up the difference; hence the

Church has a greater awareness of security and rectitude than does the individual within the Church. This knowledge extends to the infallibility of her prevailing spiritual leader when he speaks *ex cathedra* in the name of the whole Church. The Church knows this; she sees how it happens; and, nonetheless, what has happened remains ultimately mysterious; it belongs to the elevation that the Lord accomplishes in her. Out of the same mystery, the sacraments that the Church administers can administer, not only a transient and relative life, but an absolute life that issues from God's will to perfect. God is at work. The demands that God places in the Church are a part of this original work. At work, God sends to the Church, to the individual, or to the communion of saints what is required for their answer, and this is always bestowed by making excessive demands of natural man. But God gives, in addition, what distinguishes the answer from an absolute excessive demand. Thus, the man who accepts a task from God is elevated beyond his own boundaries by the Church and by God himself—beyond his own time and beyond his own finitude. Each sacrament is a sign that eternity exists and that God is present. The presence of God is a sign that he has sent both demand and fulfillment. And yet God accepts the responsibility for his invitation in such a way that man remains jointly responsible and is able to form his answer, in faith, out of a personal feeling of responsibility. He remains free to refuse. But this refusal, being contrary to the Son's will with regard to the Father, will leave its trace in the individual. He will be moved away from his place in a living relationship with God, and part of his talent, of his ability to answer, of his readiness, withers away, being neither in use nor on alert. He constructs himself out of his faculty of reason, which is no longer vivified by grace or imbued with the desire for self-gift but has become an organ incapable of perception, which rejects God's invitation and constantly discovers and invents reasons to make credible the notion that God's call is an illusion. It is the Church's task to lead to the Bridegroom the people whom he needs. The Church therefore becomes jointly responsible for the people's rejection of God, albeit in varying degrees, but with the constant reproach of having not sufficiently kept obedient watch over the vocations within her.

The individual is responsible for his Yes and for his No. An answer is due as soon as God demands it, and this is proper to the responsibility. The Christian remains free. But as a free man, he is bound in a higher way by his faith. He is bound to say Yes, but within this bond he always remains free to do so. He has to know in an objective way that he has heard an objective call that he must answer in an objective way. He has to come to terms with the call, and in doing so his responsibility remains alert.

And yet he is not alone in having been questioned like this, for God questions him as a member of the Church; the call itself belongs to the communion of saints. The communion of saints has a joint responsibility because this bond exists. The individual is meant to find in the communion of saints the place where he obtains the certainty of having heard correctly and where he stands on the verge of answering correctly. He may possess a subjective certainty about his vocation and say Yes from the bottom of a heart filled with the readiness to make a gift of self, but, even still, the Church cooperates in his Yes. For the Church holds in her hand that into which he is binding himself, even when he is joining a new foundation. Had he said Yes and his task nonetheless still not unfolded, the fault would have lain with the Church for not having offered herself to him in a way that allowed him to find his path in her. Insofar as she is meant to order the path and the place of those who are called, she is called with them and thus has to accept her living share of responsibility before God. The individual's freely given answer is accompanied by the possibilities that the Church has to offer him: the one who is called is fitted into the communion of saints in a new way, but on a marked path that is a path inside the Church and comparable to the paths along which the saints of the Church have hitherto stepped and walked. Considered in this light, the Church's responsibility grows still further: the Church is responsible for ensuring that that toward which the person who has been called is directed is kept ready for him as a precautionary measure. She cannot, therefore, make decisions that have only momentary validity; but rather, her decision must show new paths for the future of her members and offer them open possibilities; indeed, she must make decisions that take into account anticipated new instances of letting her members hear God and, thus, new unexpected vocations. This is what makes the Church a mother. In this, she lives, as Mary did before her meeting with the angel, in a readiness that made possible the Son's path on earth. Similarly, paths are made possible by the Church out of her readiness to hide within her those who have been chosen and the tasks they have been given. The bride is maternal even before she has become a mother in the sense of bearing: it is a motherliness that originates from her founding because fruitfulness is her original characteristic, as exemplified in the boundless fruitfulness of the Mother of the Lord.

XI

MAN'S ANSWER

Man's answer can be as manifold as men themselves; and yet, when the answer is an assent, it amounts to just one answer. The Son receives the answer and returns it to the Father in his own answer. The first disciples heard an entirely terse word of invitation, but, each time it was heard, it required their full commitment. They followed the best and the worst that they could. A good many doubtless did not know at the start what it was they were doing; nonetheless, they went in spite of their lack of understanding, and this was an expression of their faith. In the end, they stayed. Anyone who wanted to follow the Lord but wanted to know what his own position was as he went—predicting each and every step with specifications in hand to account for each and every freedom, reprieve, service, loss, failure, and sacrifice—would have no idea of what a gift of self really is. Not knowing what is to come is the fundamental prerequisite for a right answer to God's invitation. Meanwhile, the Lord takes over the believer's knowledge once and for all in the name of the triune God. When he said on earth as man that "of that day or that hour no one knows", this not only referred to his and to our death, but it covered the whole of life in him, it encompassed each self-denial as well as each joy, each assent as well as each failure. It included everything. And everything played out at a level on which the Christian is placed by his faith and his Yes (the two become inextricable), in a sphere of the triune God where clarity, understanding, and the will of the Father prevail as the fundamental rules.

Man is therefore invited to give his answer into a bond that has its prototype in the bond that links the three Persons in God. A man making his stumbling attempt at discipleship will notice that, whenever he takes a false step, an invisible hand will again and again pick him up and, moreover, lead him on without tiring, almost as if God had not noticed anything at all and were counting on the strength of the man's weak Yes and considered it to be wholly sufficient. Of course, when Peter was asked three times, "Do you love me?" he had to experience the Lord's reminder of his threefold denial. Nonetheless, he did not have to mention it but merely to draw its consequences into his love. However, this does not merely concern Peter's goodwill. The question, "Do you love me?" means something infinitely more demanding because, from the outset, what is meant is a level of love that is the love of the triune God— in the Church, it is "more than personal", official love. This is what the Lord now demands of Peter. Peter answers in the name of, and together with, the grazing sheep, and the Lord hears the answer of the entire flock in the answer of the appointed shepherd. Peter commits, not only himself, but everyone else with him. Thus, through his institution of the Church, the Son has created a new form of discipleship: the answer of the individual is now given under the joint responsibility of the whole Church. This does not necessarily signify a shared knowledge; for the desire to know has to disappear as much as possible from the act of saying Yes. The Lord wants an answer of faith. It will be a matter for the Holy Spirit to place as much insight into this answer as he sees fit. The one to whom the invitation has been given is like a little child who gives his hand to his mother in order to cross a threshold. The child does not need to know what awaits him in the next room. He is taken by the hand of his mother, just as the Christian is taken by the hand of the Church.

The person who says No robs, not only himself, but also the Church of the grace of his Yes. His path, whether it is splendid or very much weighed down by his refusal, has forfeited a fullness that cannot be imagined however painful its absence. He has lost an infinite amount, yet he has no more idea of how much he has lost than the person who says Yes has of how much he is gaining. The limits of personality are immediately surpassed, for the Church experiences such a considerable share in the increase or in the withdrawal of grace—as befits the answer that

has been given. There is no way of seeing histori-
cally what would have happened had all who were
called said Yes. Likewise, there is no way of seeing
theologically, since what the Church lacks in assent
contributes to a damage that takes effect throughout her entire life in the here and now. Ultimately,
the Church is, not the sum of her members, but
rather something far more extensive, which sinks its
roots within all Christians and, furthermore, is so
caught up with her bridal quality that what is essential to it cannot be stated. Nonetheless, she is represented so much in all the answers given by those
who say Yes that her riches are increased by every
one of them: her richness in insights and formula-
tions, but above all her richness in her essential being. Although no individual Christian can reshape
the face of the Church, one Christian can nonetheless be involved quite essentially in her expression, in
her facial gestures. This has nothing to do with opin-
ions. God has distinguished all missions so sharply
from one another that the loss of one or many is
as bad as the crumbling of mosaic stones from an
image. One could sketch an image of the sanctity of
the Church and establish the missing hues—the loss
of each individual Yes—with some accuracy. However, it would be impossible to say what would have
become of the Church had all the pieces remained
in place. Missions are hidden so deeply in God that,

for the most part, their course cannot be followed nor their outlines traced nor their effects foreseen.

∽

When the Lord established his Church, his Mother was still alive. The highest love that can bind two people to one another prevailed between them, a love that is both God's love for his creature and the believer's love for his Redeemer. This love is therefore both a human and an ecclesial love. When the Son of God emerges as the Bridegroom, and Mary becomes the template for the Church-bride, human love and the love proper to faith are elevated to a state that bestows the highest objectivity upon them. Mary loves her Son, not only as the one who has been born of her, but also as her neighbor in accordance with his commandment of love. It is arguably not difficult to love one's own son in the sense of a Christian love of neighbor, especially when the love has been given so completely and there can be no possibility of it being disappointed. It can be difficult, however, to perceive love as a commandment when it is fulfilled with such perfect spontaneity, naturalness, and reciprocity. It is thus difficult to apprehend as an objective "you must" something that is experienced as a subjective "you may" and as an innermost need. But this transformation is simultaneously a confirmation that this is the right path. The yearning becomes the rule, not as a concession to the Mother from the Son, but as a confirmation of the rectitude of her life. She is so right that she is elevated to become the rule: the unique is to become the repeated, and, in her love, the one person is to represent the Church.

Official, ecclesial love and spontaneous, personal love complete one another out of this ultimate example. But this is where the difficulties begin even for the disciples. Even the apostles—who in part (for instance, John) know of the relation between Mary and her Son and recognize in ecclesial love the mirror of their reciprocal love—as mere men are not capable of as much as the Mother of the Lord in her unique grace. Other apostles who did not have such a clear image as did John of the relationship between Mother and Son, and saw above all the Son and his teachings in the emerging Church, might well have put in more effort in following the path of pure adoration and love of neighbor—effort in the active as well as in the contemplative life. Perhaps they did not recognize so clearly the divine sublimity of the Lord, or they felt themselves alienated; they would have liked to have penetrated what is mysterious and could not; they constantly found themselves placed before puzzles that they were urgently supposed to solve although the Lord did not solve them in the meantime. Notwithstanding, these apostles are the Church as well, just as much as John and (in a special sense) the Mother; for the Church is not meant to remain a mere idea but should be embodied in men, just as they are. But this is where the trouble begins, right at the center of the Church; the Church's troubles *as* Church, but also the troubles of the individual (however well-intentioned he may be) who belongs to the Church and is to represent her. For, from the outset, representation is, not only an official representation, but also the representation of the individual, of the one who has been personally sent. And what is represented is that which the Lord has given to his Church to take with her—that which is objective, becomes more and more clear over the course of centuries, and is detached from the individual representative. Only in Mary does this become a perfect reality in the subject. All others look to her as the ideal but without ever totally reaching it. Peter remains forever aware of who he formerly was and of his threefold denial. His appointment as shepherd required his answer, "You know that I love you." And this answer was already ecclesial and official because, had it been spontaneous and personal, it would have been insufficient. Office and personal discipleship complete one another in the answer of the Church.

Consequently, on the path of discipleship the personal increasingly assumes ecclesial, objective characteristics. An individual comes out of love for the Lord, stays with him, and ultimately does what he commands. At the start is a very personal insight into God's call and the decision to answer him. What comes afterward is a test at a level that is so thoroughly that of the Lord that it is no longer intelligible to the one who follows. Believing, hoping, and loving, he sets off on a path that is marked by ecclesial faith, hope, and love, almost as if anyone who loves the Lord must travel the world, not with his own face, but with the one that has been given to him by the Lord; he must bear characteristics that are no longer his own but, from a distance, recall the Lord and, as it were, permit the Father to recognize the face of his disciple through the Son. This given countenance—the face of discipleship—is the objective countenance of the Church. In the same way, what the disciple does, even if it seems spontaneous, is an objective deed of the Church. The believer is constantly transported into the state that the bridal relationship requires, just as the Church is constantly conformed to the Lord in order that he might fetch new answers from her at any time. The Church finds herself in a state of doing what she does; but she finds herself no less in a state of letting deeds be brought forth by the Lord, that is, the state of "letting it be done". There is no moment in which the Church's own deeds can be clearly deciphered any more than there is a precisely recognizable place in her deeds where she "lets it be done"; instead, there is a confluence of both in obedience to the Lord.

In order to comprehend the life of the Church, it is necessary to separate the Lord's life into two phases: first, from his conception to his death on the Cross; secondly, from his Resurrection to his Ascension. The Eucharist forms the bridge between these two phases. The Eucharist is instituted before the Passion, but the Church first celebrates it as her own sacrifice following the Resurrection. The eucharistic Body shows its most profound significance as the bridge between suffering and Resurrection, above and beyond death: it is into the Body that the bread is changed, into the Blood that the wine is changed.

But it is the same humanity of the Lord that was placed in the first phase between the Mother's "let it be done" and his own "let it be done" on the Cross. And between them the Lord established his Church, which has his true bodily presence at her center. Without his existence among these men who represent the beginnings of the Church, they would represent a totally futureless figment: a few devotees who go along with it for a while without a proper

understanding but who then, as little men full of
hesitation and shortcomings, leave their master in
his suffering. The whole thing is like a human shell
that only gets its core from the presence of the Lord
and his divine Spirit. Only the Mother's "letting it
be done" at the start is equivalent to an infinite hope
that will find its fulfillment when the Son comes;
but she, too, would stand outside of the Son as an
empty husk. And thus the Son foresees how much
men need his bodily presence in order to take any
path that can count as in any way Christian. But
he also foresees his own death. He must bear the
thought of his own death in a very human way in
order to experience his brothers' position and to se-
cure his divine-human presence among them in relation to it. It is here that all the sacraments come
into being: first and foremost the Eucharist with regard to the Cross and the sacrament of Reconciliation as the first gift from the Cross. The word of
absolution, however, is meant to make the believer
capable of receiving the Lord in all the forms of his
presence: as the word of prayer and love of neighbor
and as the eucharistic word in Flesh and Blood.

But all this is confirmed by the Holy Spirit. In
the second phase, as the Lord prepares to leave the
earth, the sacraments come alive in the Church. The
eucharistic life of the Lord is sunk into her above all
so that when he ascends into heaven he withdraws
nothing from her. Now the Mother's hope can be

fulfilled, not only in the Son's being, but equally in the Church as well. And it is no longer the Virgin alone who gives her Yes but, together with her, the new Christian Church that has been founded and is coming into being. Henceforth, the faithful have the certainty that the Church's answer to the infinite God means that she puts herself at his disposal completely in a way that has been pre-formed in Mary's Yes, fulfilled in the life of the Son, and co-fulfilled by the Church as she administers the sacraments in the way of life that the Lord gives her. It is no longer the Yes of an individual virgin who promises and makes a gift of everything. It is the Yes of a safely founded community that is blessed with every promise. It is a Yes that bridges, a string on which ecclesial happenings are strung like pearls—the forms of the ecclesial unity of life that bestow upon all the faithful a safe place in the Church. The Yes of the individual is no longer endangered by his weaknesses; it is fulfilled in the Church. This fulfillment proceeds through the Mother's Yes, through the whole of the Lord's human life, through his entire ecclesial life from the Cross until his Ascension, and he takes it with him into heaven in order that through the fullness of the Spirit it might be brought to men at Pentecost in a living and present memory. The Son has taken the Yes of his weak Church up on high with him, and in the ten days before Pentecost it is subject to an examination by the triune God. And

when the Spirit descends, he brings fullness from
heaven, the visible evidence of the Yes that is now
capable of enduring the millennia and of again and
again being expressed anew and personally, but also
again and again anonymously and ecclesially. That
does not mean that the word that the Mother gave
is in any way diminished, for she gave her word
when she was alone with the angel in a reality that
at first only she could experience, although it was
so concrete that it led to the Incarnation of the Son.
Through her Yes, the Mother has allowed a piece
of heaven to become a Church that encompasses the
world. Thus, hers is no longer either a lonely Yes
or a Yes to an excessive personal demand. Instead,
it is the communion of saints' Yes before the triune God, a Yes in the certainty that the incarnate
God has given her and in the steadfastness out of
which he himself said, "Not my will, but thine, be
done." It is the indivisible Yes that bridges every situation and gives the living life of the Lord to all the
faithful.

Hence the answer that the Father now receives is
a single and yet multiform answer. He does not hear
it as the voice of an isolated individual; for the individual is always invited by the Son to satisfy the
demands of the Father with the strength of the Holy
Spirit, in the unity of the Son who lives on in the
communion of saints, and with the definitive where-
withal of the Mother's Yes. The answer is ecclesial.

And God receives it in the Spirit out of which he has formed the Son's mission. And he receives it as the Son's return to heaven having suffered the Cross. This reception means that the Father places the whole of heaven at the Son's disposal, that he receives the Yes of men included in that of the Son in heaven, and that he bestows upon it the value of eternity. The whole concrete Yes of the man who wants what God wants and who places himself at God's disposal is received in heaven as a word that has been completed: a word that can do nothing other than offer a human existence; a weak human word that becomes an eternal word, already spoken by the Son, confirmed by the believer, and bestowed with such strength that in a moment it becomes eternity and the boundedness that is ultimately characteristic of human words is elevated unto God.

If the Son is the Word of the Father, he is consequently the witness to the Father's infinity and has come to give this eternity meaning on earth and, through his own sacrifice, to place all men under obligation to the Father. He found the perfect fulfillment of his own life in his Mother's Yes, for she is pre-redeemed and has received the grace and dignity to join in uttering the valid word, in the Son, that he himself will utter. He has fulfilled himself in this word just as she has fulfilled herself through it; he has given this word the significance of the Church's eternal Yes to the triune God. He has thus made it capable of eternity. But he has not left it as an isolated word; rather, he has given it the vocal resonance of all the faithful. The Father receives it filled in this way: as the Son's word together with those who are his. Nothing can happen to this word in the individual believer or in the Church except that it be used to the ever greater glorification of God. It does not ring out from some corner or other where one could behold and judge the glory of God; instead, it is seized by the strength of God and raised on high and returned from heaven—a thousand, indeed a million times amplified—as a witness to eternity. It is now a word that has power, not only to embody God's voice on earth, but also to reshape the face of the world as God intends it to be. God takes the word of man from him, and it experiences the infinity of heaven. When man reencounters it—that is, when he finds his answer complete in Christ —he experiences in it God's greatness and recognizes how great the power of the Father's Word in the triune God really is; what God intended when he created the world and man in the Word; how the Son, becoming man, stood by him; how the Spirit accompanied the work of the Father and Son and completes it; and, finally, how everything redounds to the best for those who love God: in heaven. Their Yes is the opening onto the eternal vision of the Father, Son, and Spirit's eternal life.